45 Cheesecake Recipes for Home

By: Kelly Johnson

Table of Contents

- Classic New York Cheesecake
- Chocolate Swirl Cheesecake
- Strawberry Cheesecake
- Blueberry Cheesecake
- Raspberry White Chocolate Cheesecake
- Lemon Cheesecake
- Key Lime Cheesecake
- Salted Caramel Cheesecake
- Oreo Cheesecake
- Peanut Butter Cup Cheesecake
- Tiramisu Cheesecake
- Pumpkin Cheesecake
- Cherry Almond Cheesecake
- Mint Chocolate Chip Cheesecake
- Pecan Pie Cheesecake
- Cookies and Cream Cheesecake
- Red Velvet Cheesecake
- Mocha Cheesecake
- Maple Pecan Cheesecake
- Banana Foster Cheesecake
- Pistachio Cheesecake
- Coconut Lime Cheesecake
- White Chocolate Raspberry Cheesecake
- Espresso Cheesecake
- Strawberry Shortcake Cheesecake
- Almond Joy Cheesecake
- Black Forest Cheesecake
- Caramel Apple Cheesecake
- Chocolate Hazelnut Cheesecake
- Mango Passionfruit Cheesecake
- S'mores Cheesecake
- Raspberry Lemonade Cheesecake
- Turtle Cheesecake
- Almond Amaretto Cheesecake
- Chocolate Covered Strawberry Cheesecake

- Brownie Bottom Cheesecake
- Snickers Cheesecake
- Cinnamon Roll Cheesecake
- Chocolate Mousse Cheesecake
- Blueberry Lemon Cheesecake Bars
- Marble Cheesecake
- Raspberry Cheesecake Ice Cream
- Pineapple Upside-Down Cheesecake
- Matcha Green Tea Cheesecake
- Fig and Honey Cheesecake

Classic New York Cheesecake

Ingredients:

For the Crust:

- 1 1/2 cups graham cracker crumbs
- 1/4 cup melted unsalted butter
- 2 tablespoons granulated sugar

For the Cheesecake Filling:

- 4 packages (32 ounces) cream cheese, softened
- 1 1/4 cups granulated sugar
- 1 teaspoon vanilla extract
- 4 large eggs, room temperature
- 1 cup sour cream
- 1/4 cup all-purpose flour
- Pinch of salt

Instructions:

1. Preheat the Oven:

- Preheat your oven to 325°F (163°C). Grease the bottom and sides of a 9-inch springform pan.

2. Prepare the Crust:

- In a medium bowl, mix graham cracker crumbs, melted butter, and sugar until the crumbs are evenly coated. Press the mixture into the bottom of the prepared springform pan to create an even crust.

3. Bake the Crust:

- Bake the crust in the preheated oven for about 10 minutes or until it sets. Remove from the oven and let it cool while preparing the filling.

4. Prepare the Cheesecake Filling:

    - In a large mixing bowl, beat the softened cream cheese until smooth using an electric mixer.
    - Add sugar and vanilla extract to the cream cheese, and continue beating until well combined.
    - Add eggs one at a time, beating well after each addition.
    - Mix in sour cream, flour, and a pinch of salt. Beat until the batter is smooth and creamy.

5. Pour Filling into the Crust:

    - Pour the cheesecake filling over the baked crust in the springform pan.

6. Bake the Cheesecake:

    - Bake in the preheated oven for about 1 hour or until the center is set and the top is lightly browned.

7. Cool and Refrigerate:

    - Allow the cheesecake to cool in the pan on a wire rack. Once it reaches room temperature, cover and refrigerate for at least 4 hours or overnight.

8. Serve:

    - Before serving, run a knife around the edge of the pan to loosen the cheesecake. Remove the sides of the springform pan.
    - Slice and serve the Classic New York Cheesecake as is or with your favorite fruit topping.

Note: For best results, let the cheesecake chill in the refrigerator for an extended period to allow the flavors to meld and the texture to set properly.

Enjoy this classic and creamy New York Cheesecake!

Chocolate Swirl Cheesecake

Ingredients:

For the Crust:

- 1 1/2 cups chocolate cookie crumbs (such as chocolate graham crackers or chocolate sandwich cookies)
- 1/4 cup melted unsalted butter
- 2 tablespoons granulated sugar

For the Cheesecake Filling:

- 4 packages (32 ounces) cream cheese, softened
- 1 1/4 cups granulated sugar
- 1 teaspoon vanilla extract
- 4 large eggs, room temperature
- 1 cup sour cream
- 1/4 cup all-purpose flour
- Pinch of salt

For the Chocolate Swirl:

- 4 ounces semisweet chocolate, chopped
- 2 tablespoons unsalted butter
- 2 tablespoons cocoa powder
- 2 tablespoons powdered sugar

Instructions:

1. Preheat the Oven:

- Preheat your oven to 325°F (163°C). Grease the bottom and sides of a 9-inch springform pan.

2. Prepare the Crust:

- In a medium bowl, mix chocolate cookie crumbs, melted butter, and sugar until the crumbs are evenly coated. Press the mixture into the bottom of the prepared springform pan to create an even crust.

3. Bake the Crust:

- Bake the crust in the preheated oven for about 10 minutes or until it sets. Remove from the oven and let it cool while preparing the filling.

4. Prepare the Cheesecake Filling:

- In a large mixing bowl, beat the softened cream cheese until smooth using an electric mixer.
- Add sugar and vanilla extract to the cream cheese, and continue beating until well combined.
- Add eggs one at a time, beating well after each addition.
- Mix in sour cream, flour, and a pinch of salt. Beat until the batter is smooth and creamy.

5. Prepare the Chocolate Swirl:

- In a small saucepan, melt the chocolate and butter over low heat. Stir in cocoa powder and powdered sugar until smooth.

6. Swirl the Chocolate Mixture:

- Pour the cheesecake batter over the baked crust in the springform pan.
- Drop spoonfuls of the chocolate mixture onto the cheesecake batter. Use a knife or skewer to create swirl patterns by gently running it through the chocolate and cheesecake layers.

7. Bake the Cheesecake:

- Bake in the preheated oven for about 1 hour or until the center is set and the top is lightly browned.

8. Cool and Refrigerate:

- Allow the cheesecake to cool in the pan on a wire rack. Once it reaches room temperature, cover and refrigerate for at least 4 hours or overnight.

9. Serve:

- Before serving, run a knife around the edge of the pan to loosen the cheesecake. Remove the sides of the springform pan.
- Slice and serve the Chocolate Swirl Cheesecake, optionally with a dollop of whipped cream or a drizzle of chocolate sauce.

Enjoy this decadent and visually stunning Chocolate Swirl Cheesecake!

Strawberry Cheesecake

Ingredients:

For the Crust:

- 1 1/2 cups graham cracker crumbs
- 1/4 cup melted unsalted butter
- 2 tablespoons granulated sugar

For the Cheesecake Filling:

- 4 packages (32 ounces) cream cheese, softened
- 1 1/4 cups granulated sugar
- 1 teaspoon vanilla extract
- 4 large eggs, room temperature
- 1 cup sour cream
- 1/4 cup all-purpose flour
- Pinch of salt

For the Strawberry Topping:

- 2 cups fresh strawberries, hulled and sliced
- 1/4 cup granulated sugar
- 1 tablespoon lemon juice
- 1 tablespoon cornstarch (optional for thickening)

Instructions:

1. Preheat the Oven:

- Preheat your oven to 325°F (163°C). Grease the bottom and sides of a 9-inch springform pan.

2. Prepare the Crust:

- In a medium bowl, mix graham cracker crumbs, melted butter, and sugar until the crumbs are evenly coated. Press the mixture into the bottom of the prepared springform pan to create an even crust.

3. Bake the Crust:

    - Bake the crust in the preheated oven for about 10 minutes or until it sets. Remove from the oven and let it cool while preparing the filling.

4. Prepare the Cheesecake Filling:

    - In a large mixing bowl, beat the softened cream cheese until smooth using an electric mixer.
    - Add sugar and vanilla extract to the cream cheese, and continue beating until well combined.
    - Add eggs one at a time, beating well after each addition.
    - Mix in sour cream, flour, and a pinch of salt. Beat until the batter is smooth and creamy.

5. Pour Filling onto the Crust:

    - Pour the cheesecake filling over the baked crust in the springform pan.

6. Bake the Cheesecake:

    - Bake in the preheated oven for about 1 hour or until the center is set and the top is lightly browned.

7. Cool and Refrigerate:

    - Allow the cheesecake to cool in the pan on a wire rack. Once it reaches room temperature, cover and refrigerate for at least 4 hours or overnight.

8. Prepare the Strawberry Topping:

    - In a saucepan, combine sliced strawberries, sugar, and lemon juice. Cook over medium heat until the strawberries release their juices and become syrupy. If you

prefer a thicker topping, mix cornstarch with a little water and add it to the strawberry mixture, stirring until thickened.
- Let the strawberry topping cool before spreading it over the chilled cheesecake.

9. Serve:

- Before serving, run a knife around the edge of the pan to loosen the cheesecake. Remove the sides of the springform pan.
- Spoon the strawberry topping over the cheesecake.

10. Enjoy:

- Slice and enjoy this delightful Strawberry Cheesecake!

This strawberry cheesecake is a perfect blend of creamy richness and fruity freshness.

It's a classic dessert that's sure to be a hit!

Blueberry Cheesecake

Ingredients:

For the Crust:

- 1 1/2 cups graham cracker crumbs
- 1/4 cup melted unsalted butter
- 2 tablespoons granulated sugar

For the Cheesecake Filling:

- 4 packages (32 ounces) cream cheese, softened
- 1 1/4 cups granulated sugar
- 1 teaspoon vanilla extract
- 4 large eggs, room temperature
- 1 cup sour cream
- 1/4 cup all-purpose flour
- Pinch of salt

For the Blueberry Topping:

- 2 cups fresh or frozen blueberries
- 1/2 cup granulated sugar
- 2 tablespoons lemon juice
- 1 tablespoon cornstarch (optional for thickening)

Instructions:

1. Preheat the Oven:

- Preheat your oven to 325°F (163°C). Grease the bottom and sides of a 9-inch springform pan.

2. Prepare the Crust:

- In a medium bowl, mix graham cracker crumbs, melted butter, and sugar until the crumbs are evenly coated. Press the mixture into the bottom of the prepared springform pan to create an even crust.

3. Bake the Crust:

    - Bake the crust in the preheated oven for about 10 minutes or until it sets. Remove from the oven and let it cool while preparing the filling.

4. Prepare the Cheesecake Filling:

    - In a large mixing bowl, beat the softened cream cheese until smooth using an electric mixer.
    - Add sugar and vanilla extract to the cream cheese, and continue beating until well combined.
    - Add eggs one at a time, beating well after each addition.
    - Mix in sour cream, flour, and a pinch of salt. Beat until the batter is smooth and creamy.

5. Pour Filling onto the Crust:

    - Pour the cheesecake filling over the baked crust in the springform pan.

6. Bake the Cheesecake:

    - Bake in the preheated oven for about 1 hour or until the center is set and the top is lightly browned.

7. Cool and Refrigerate:

    - Allow the cheesecake to cool in the pan on a wire rack. Once it reaches room temperature, cover and refrigerate for at least 4 hours or overnight.

8. Prepare the Blueberry Topping:

    - In a saucepan, combine blueberries, sugar, and lemon juice. Cook over medium heat until the blueberries release their juices and become syrupy. If you prefer a

thicker topping, mix cornstarch with a little water and add it to the blueberry mixture, stirring until thickened.
- Let the blueberry topping cool before spreading it over the chilled cheesecake.

9. Serve:

- Before serving, run a knife around the edge of the pan to loosen the cheesecake. Remove the sides of the springform pan.
- Spoon the blueberry topping over the cheesecake.

10. Enjoy:

- Slice and enjoy this delightful Blueberry Cheesecake!

This blueberry cheesecake combines the creamy goodness of cheesecake with the sweetness of a blueberry topping. It's a perfect dessert for any occasion!

Raspberry White Chocolate Cheesecake

Ingredients:

For the Crust:

- 1 1/2 cups graham cracker crumbs
- 1/4 cup melted unsalted butter
- 2 tablespoons granulated sugar

For the Cheesecake Filling:

- 4 packages (32 ounces) cream cheese, softened
- 1 1/4 cups granulated sugar
- 1 teaspoon vanilla extract
- 4 large eggs, room temperature
- 1 cup sour cream
- 1/4 cup all-purpose flour
- Pinch of salt

For the Raspberry White Chocolate Swirl:

- 1 cup fresh or frozen raspberries
- 1/4 cup granulated sugar
- 1 tablespoon cornstarch
- 1/2 cup white chocolate chips, melted

Instructions:

1. Preheat the Oven:

- Preheat your oven to 325°F (163°C). Grease the bottom and sides of a 9-inch springform pan.

2. Prepare the Crust:

- In a medium bowl, mix graham cracker crumbs, melted butter, and sugar until the crumbs are evenly coated. Press the mixture into the bottom of the prepared springform pan to create an even crust.

3. Bake the Crust:

- Bake the crust in the preheated oven for about 10 minutes or until it sets. Remove from the oven and let it cool while preparing the filling.

4. Prepare the Cheesecake Filling:

- In a large mixing bowl, beat the softened cream cheese until smooth using an electric mixer.
- Add sugar and vanilla extract to the cream cheese, and continue beating until well combined.
- Add eggs one at a time, beating well after each addition.
- Mix in sour cream, flour, and a pinch of salt. Beat until the batter is smooth and creamy.

5. Prepare the Raspberry White Chocolate Swirl:

- In a small saucepan, combine raspberries, sugar, and cornstarch. Cook over medium heat until the raspberries release their juices and become syrupy. Strain the mixture to remove seeds.
- Melt the white chocolate chips in a separate bowl.
- Gently fold the raspberry sauce into the melted white chocolate to create a swirl mixture.

6. Assemble the Cheesecake:

- Pour the cheesecake filling over the baked crust in the springform pan.
- Drop spoonfuls of the raspberry white chocolate swirl mixture over the cheesecake batter. Use a knife or skewer to create swirl patterns by gently running it through the raspberry and white chocolate layers.

7. Bake the Cheesecake:

- Bake in the preheated oven for about 1 hour or until the center is set and the top is lightly browned.

8. Cool and Refrigerate:

- Allow the cheesecake to cool in the pan on a wire rack. Once it reaches room temperature, cover and refrigerate for at least 4 hours or overnight.

9. Serve:

- Before serving, run a knife around the edge of the pan to loosen the cheesecake. Remove the sides of the springform pan.

10. Enjoy:

- Slice and enjoy this decadent Raspberry White Chocolate Cheesecake!

This cheesecake offers a perfect balance of creamy cheesecake, sweet white chocolate, and the fruity freshness of raspberries. It's a delightful treat for any dessert lover.

Lemon Cheesecake

Ingredients:

For the Crust:

- 1 1/2 cups graham cracker crumbs
- 1/4 cup melted unsalted butter
- 2 tablespoons granulated sugar

For the Cheesecake Filling:

- 4 packages (32 ounces) cream cheese, softened
- 1 1/4 cups granulated sugar
- 1 teaspoon vanilla extract
- 4 large eggs, room temperature
- 1 cup sour cream
- 1/4 cup all-purpose flour
- Zest of 2 lemons
- 1/4 cup fresh lemon juice
- Pinch of salt

For the Lemon Curd Topping:

- 1/2 cup fresh lemon juice
- 1/2 cup granulated sugar
- 2 large eggs
- 1/4 cup unsalted butter, cubed
- Zest of 1 lemon

Instructions:

1. Preheat the Oven:

- Preheat your oven to 325°F (163°C). Grease the bottom and sides of a 9-inch springform pan.

2. Prepare the Crust:

- In a medium bowl, mix graham cracker crumbs, melted butter, and sugar until the crumbs are evenly coated. Press the mixture into the bottom of the prepared springform pan to create an even crust.

3. Bake the Crust:

- Bake the crust in the preheated oven for about 10 minutes or until it sets. Remove from the oven and let it cool while preparing the filling.

4. Prepare the Cheesecake Filling:

- In a large mixing bowl, beat the softened cream cheese until smooth using an electric mixer.
- Add sugar and vanilla extract to the cream cheese, and continue beating until well combined.
- Add eggs one at a time, beating well after each addition.
- Mix in sour cream, flour, lemon zest, lemon juice, and a pinch of salt. Beat until the batter is smooth and creamy.

5. Pour Filling onto the Crust:

- Pour the lemon-flavored cheesecake filling over the baked crust in the springform pan.

6. Bake the Cheesecake:

- Bake in the preheated oven for about 1 hour or until the center is set and the top is lightly browned.

7. Cool and Refrigerate:

- Allow the cheesecake to cool in the pan on a wire rack. Once it reaches room temperature, cover and refrigerate for at least 4 hours or overnight.

8. Prepare the Lemon Curd Topping:

- In a saucepan, whisk together lemon juice, sugar, and eggs over medium heat. Add butter and continue whisking until the mixture thickens and coats the back of a spoon. Stir in lemon zest.
- Allow the lemon curd to cool, then spread it over the chilled cheesecake.

9. Serve:

- Before serving, run a knife around the edge of the pan to loosen the cheesecake. Remove the sides of the springform pan.

10. Enjoy:

- Slice and enjoy this refreshing Lemon Cheesecake with a luscious lemon curd topping!

This lemon-infused cheesecake is a burst of citrusy flavor, perfect for those who love the refreshing taste of lemons in their desserts.

Key Lime Cheesecake

Ingredients:

For the Crust:

- 1 1/2 cups graham cracker crumbs
- 1/4 cup melted unsalted butter
- 2 tablespoons granulated sugar

For the Cheesecake Filling:

- 4 packages (32 ounces) cream cheese, softened
- 1 1/4 cups granulated sugar
- 1 teaspoon vanilla extract
- 4 large eggs, room temperature
- 1 cup sour cream
- 1/4 cup all-purpose flour
- Zest of 4 key limes
- 1/2 cup key lime juice (freshly squeezed)

For the Key Lime Whipped Cream:

- 1 cup heavy cream
- 2 tablespoons powdered sugar
- 1 tablespoon key lime juice
- Zest of 1 key lime

Instructions:

1. Preheat the Oven:

- Preheat your oven to 325°F (163°C). Grease the bottom and sides of a 9-inch springform pan.

2. Prepare the Crust:

- In a medium bowl, mix graham cracker crumbs, melted butter, and sugar until the crumbs are evenly coated. Press the mixture into the bottom of the prepared springform pan to create an even crust.

3. Bake the Crust:

- Bake the crust in the preheated oven for about 10 minutes or until it sets. Remove from the oven and let it cool while preparing the filling.

4. Prepare the Cheesecake Filling:

- In a large mixing bowl, beat the softened cream cheese until smooth using an electric mixer.
- Add sugar and vanilla extract to the cream cheese, and continue beating until well combined.
- Add eggs one at a time, beating well after each addition.
- Mix in sour cream, flour, key lime zest, and key lime juice. Beat until the batter is smooth and creamy.

5. Pour Filling onto the Crust:

- Pour the key lime-flavored cheesecake filling over the baked crust in the springform pan.

6. Bake the Cheesecake:

- Bake in the preheated oven for about 1 hour or until the center is set and the top is lightly browned.

7. Cool and Refrigerate:

- Allow the cheesecake to cool in the pan on a wire rack. Once it reaches room temperature, cover and refrigerate for at least 4 hours or overnight.

8. Prepare the Key Lime Whipped Cream:

- In a chilled bowl, whip the heavy cream until it starts to thicken. Add powdered sugar, key lime juice, and key lime zest. Continue whipping until stiff peaks form.

9. Serve:

- Before serving, run a knife around the edge of the pan to loosen the cheesecake. Remove the sides of the springform pan.
- Top the chilled cheesecake with key lime whipped cream.

10. Enjoy:

- Slice and enjoy this delightful Key Lime Cheesecake with a zesty key lime twist!

This key lime cheesecake is a refreshing and tangy dessert, perfect for those who love the unique flavor of key limes.

Salted Caramel Cheesecake

Ingredients:

For the Crust:

- 1 1/2 cups graham cracker crumbs
- 1/4 cup melted unsalted butter
- 2 tablespoons granulated sugar

For the Cheesecake Filling:

- 4 packages (32 ounces) cream cheese, softened
- 1 1/4 cups granulated sugar
- 1 teaspoon vanilla extract
- 4 large eggs, room temperature
- 1 cup sour cream
- 1/4 cup all-purpose flour
- Pinch of salt

For the Salted Caramel Sauce:

- 1 cup granulated sugar
- 6 tablespoons unsalted butter, cut into pieces
- 1/2 cup heavy cream
- 1 teaspoon sea salt (adjust to taste)

Instructions:

1. Preheat the Oven:

- Preheat your oven to 325°F (163°C). Grease the bottom and sides of a 9-inch springform pan.

2. Prepare the Crust:

- In a medium bowl, mix graham cracker crumbs, melted butter, and sugar until the crumbs are evenly coated. Press the mixture into the bottom of the prepared springform pan to create an even crust.

3. Bake the Crust:

- Bake the crust in the preheated oven for about 10 minutes or until it sets. Remove from the oven and let it cool while preparing the filling.

4. Prepare the Cheesecake Filling:

- In a large mixing bowl, beat the softened cream cheese until smooth using an electric mixer.
- Add sugar and vanilla extract to the cream cheese, and continue beating until well combined.
- Add eggs one at a time, beating well after each addition.
- Mix in sour cream, flour, and a pinch of salt. Beat until the batter is smooth and creamy.

5. Pour Filling onto the Crust:

- Pour the cheesecake filling over the baked crust in the springform pan.

6. Bake the Cheesecake:

- Bake in the preheated oven for about 1 hour or until the center is set and the top is lightly browned.

7. Cool and Refrigerate:

- Allow the cheesecake to cool in the pan on a wire rack. Once it reaches room temperature, cover and refrigerate for at least 4 hours or overnight.

8. Prepare the Salted Caramel Sauce:

- In a saucepan, heat granulated sugar over medium heat, stirring constantly until it melts and turns amber in color.
- Add butter to the melted sugar and stir until fully combined.
- Slowly pour in the heavy cream while stirring continuously. Be cautious, as the mixture will bubble.
- Stir in sea salt to taste. Allow the caramel sauce to cool before using.

9. Pour Salted Caramel Sauce:

- Once the cheesecake is chilled, pour the salted caramel sauce over the top, spreading it evenly.

10. Serve:

- Before serving, run a knife around the edge of the pan to loosen the cheesecake. Remove the sides of the springform pan.
- Slice and enjoy this indulgent Salted Caramel Cheesecake!

This cheesecake combines the rich creaminess of the filling with the sweet and salty goodness of homemade salted caramel sauce for a delightful treat.

Oreo Cheesecake

Ingredients:

For the Crust:

- 2 cups Oreo cookie crumbs (about 20-25 cookies)
- 1/4 cup melted unsalted butter

For the Cheesecake Filling:

- 4 packages (32 ounces) cream cheese, softened
- 1 1/4 cups granulated sugar
- 1 teaspoon vanilla extract
- 4 large eggs, room temperature
- 1 cup sour cream
- 1/4 cup all-purpose flour
- 1 cup crushed Oreo cookies

For the Oreo Whipped Cream Topping:

- 1 cup heavy cream
- 2 tablespoons powdered sugar
- 1/2 teaspoon vanilla extract
- Crushed Oreo cookies for garnish

Instructions:

1. Preheat the Oven:

- Preheat your oven to 325°F (163°C). Grease the bottom and sides of a 9-inch springform pan.

2. Prepare the Crust:

- In a bowl, combine Oreo cookie crumbs and melted butter. Press the mixture into the bottom of the prepared springform pan to create a firm crust.

3. Bake the Crust:

- Bake the crust in the preheated oven for about 10 minutes. Remove from the oven and let it cool while preparing the filling.

4. Prepare the Cheesecake Filling:

    - In a large mixing bowl, beat the softened cream cheese until smooth using an electric mixer.
    - Add sugar and vanilla extract to the cream cheese, and continue beating until well combined.
    - Add eggs one at a time, beating well after each addition.
    - Mix in sour cream, flour, and crushed Oreo cookies. Beat until the batter is smooth and creamy.

5. Pour Filling onto the Crust:

    - Pour the Oreo-flavored cheesecake filling over the baked crust in the springform pan.

6. Bake the Cheesecake:

    - Bake in the preheated oven for about 1 hour or until the center is set and the top is lightly browned.

7. Cool and Refrigerate:

    - Allow the cheesecake to cool in the pan on a wire rack. Once it reaches room temperature, cover and refrigerate for at least 4 hours or overnight.

8. Prepare the Oreo Whipped Cream Topping:

    - In a chilled bowl, whip the heavy cream until it starts to thicken. Add powdered sugar and vanilla extract. Continue whipping until stiff peaks form.

9. Spread Whipped Cream and Garnish:

    - Spread the Oreo whipped cream over the chilled cheesecake.
    - Garnish the top with additional crushed Oreo cookies.

10. Serve:

- Before serving, run a knife around the edge of the pan to loosen the cheesecake. Remove the sides of the springform pan.
- Slice and indulge in this decadent Oreo Cheesecake!

This Oreo Cheesecake is a delightful combination of creamy cheesecake filling and the irresistible flavor of Oreo cookies, making it a perfect treat for Oreo lovers!

Peanut Butter Cup Cheesecake

Ingredients:

For the Crust:

- 2 cups chocolate cookie crumbs (such as chocolate graham crackers or chocolate sandwich cookies)
- 1/2 cup melted unsalted butter

For the Cheesecake Filling:

- 4 packages (32 ounces) cream cheese, softened
- 1 1/4 cups granulated sugar
- 1 teaspoon vanilla extract
- 4 large eggs, room temperature
- 1 cup sour cream
- 1/4 cup all-purpose flour
- 1 cup creamy peanut butter
- 1 cup chopped peanut butter cups

For the Peanut Butter Ganache:

- 1/2 cup heavy cream
- 1 cup semisweet chocolate chips
- 1/2 cup creamy peanut butter

For Garnish:

- Chopped peanut butter cups

Instructions:

1. Preheat the Oven:

- Preheat your oven to 325°F (163°C). Grease the bottom and sides of a 9-inch springform pan.

2. Prepare the Crust:

    - In a bowl, mix chocolate cookie crumbs and melted butter. Press the mixture into the bottom of the prepared springform pan to create a firm crust.

3. Bake the Crust:

    - Bake the crust in the preheated oven for about 10 minutes. Remove from the oven and let it cool while preparing the filling.

4. Prepare the Cheesecake Filling:

    - In a large mixing bowl, beat the softened cream cheese until smooth using an electric mixer.
    - Add sugar and vanilla extract to the cream cheese, and continue beating until well combined.
    - Add eggs one at a time, beating well after each addition.
    - Mix in sour cream, flour, peanut butter, and chopped peanut butter cups. Beat until the batter is smooth and creamy.

5. Pour Filling onto the Crust:

    - Pour the peanut butter cup-flavored cheesecake filling over the baked crust in the springform pan.

6. Bake the Cheesecake:

    - Bake in the preheated oven for about 1 hour or until the center is set and the top is lightly browned.

7. Cool and Refrigerate:

    - Allow the cheesecake to cool in the pan on a wire rack. Once it reaches room temperature, cover and refrigerate for at least 4 hours or overnight.

8. Prepare the Peanut Butter Ganache:

   - In a saucepan, heat the heavy cream until it's just about to boil. Remove from heat and add chocolate chips and peanut butter. Stir until smooth and well combined.

9. Pour Ganache over Cheesecake:

   - Pour the peanut butter ganache over the chilled cheesecake, spreading it evenly.

10. Garnish and Serve:

    - Garnish the top with chopped peanut butter cups.
    - Before serving, run a knife around the edge of the pan to loosen the cheesecake. Remove the sides of the springform pan.
    - Slice and enjoy this indulgent Peanut Butter Cup Cheesecake!

This cheesecake is a peanut butter lover's dream, with the rich and creamy peanut butter filling complemented by the decadent peanut butter ganache and the delightful addition of peanut butter cup chunks.

Tiramisu Cheesecake

Ingredients:

For the Crust:

- 2 cups espresso-flavored ladyfinger cookie crumbs (about 24-28 ladyfingers)
- 1/2 cup melted unsalted butter

For the Cheesecake Filling:

- 4 packages (32 ounces) cream cheese, softened
- 1 1/4 cups granulated sugar
- 1 teaspoon vanilla extract
- 4 large eggs, room temperature
- 1 cup sour cream
- 1/4 cup all-purpose flour
- 1/4 cup brewed espresso or strong coffee, cooled

For the Tiramisu Topping:

- 1 cup heavy cream
- 1/4 cup powdered sugar
- 2 tablespoons cocoa powder (for dusting)
- 2 tablespoons grated chocolate or cocoa powder (for garnish)

For the Coffee Soaking Liquid:

- 1/2 cup brewed espresso or strong coffee, cooled
- 2 tablespoons coffee liqueur (optional)

Instructions:

1. Preheat the Oven:

- Preheat your oven to 325°F (163°C). Grease the bottom and sides of a 9-inch springform pan.

2. Prepare the Crust:

- In a bowl, mix espresso-flavored ladyfinger cookie crumbs and melted butter. Press the mixture into the bottom of the prepared springform pan to create a firm crust.

3. Bake the Crust:

- Bake the crust in the preheated oven for about 10 minutes. Remove from the oven and let it cool while preparing the filling.

4. Prepare the Cheesecake Filling:

- In a large mixing bowl, beat the softened cream cheese until smooth using an electric mixer.
- Add sugar and vanilla extract to the cream cheese, and continue beating until well combined.
- Add eggs one at a time, beating well after each addition.
- Mix in sour cream, flour, and brewed espresso. Beat until the batter is smooth and creamy.

5. Prepare the Coffee Soaking Liquid:

- In a small bowl, combine brewed espresso (or strong coffee) with coffee liqueur, if using.

6. Pour Filling onto the Crust:

- Pour half of the cheesecake filling over the baked crust in the springform pan.

7. Add Coffee Soaking Liquid:

- Brush half of the coffee soaking liquid over the first layer of cheesecake filling.

8. Repeat Layers:

   - Pour the remaining cheesecake filling over the first layer.
   - Brush the remaining coffee soaking liquid over the second layer.

9. Bake the Cheesecake:

   - Bake in the preheated oven for about 1 hour or until the center is set and the top is lightly browned.

10. Cool and Refrigerate:

    - Allow the cheesecake to cool in the pan on a wire rack. Once it reaches room temperature, cover and refrigerate for at least 4 hours or overnight.

11. Prepare the Tiramisu Topping:

    - In a chilled bowl, whip the heavy cream until it starts to thicken. Add powdered sugar and continue whipping until stiff peaks form.

12. Spread Whipped Cream and Garnish:

    - Spread the whipped cream over the chilled cheesecake.
    - Dust the top with cocoa powder and garnish with grated chocolate or additional cocoa powder.

13. Serve:

    - Before serving, run a knife around the edge of the pan to loosen the cheesecake. Remove the sides of the springform pan.
    - Slice and savor this delightful Tiramisu Cheesecake, reminiscent of the classic Italian dessert!

This Tiramisu Cheesecake combines the rich flavors of espresso, ladyfingers, and creamy cheesecake for a decadent and irresistible treat.

Pumpkin Cheesecake

Ingredients:

For the Crust:

- 2 cups graham cracker crumbs
- 1/2 cup melted unsalted butter
- 1/4 cup granulated sugar

For the Cheesecake Filling:

- 4 packages (32 ounces) cream cheese, softened
- 1 1/2 cups granulated sugar
- 4 large eggs, room temperature
- 1 cup canned pumpkin puree
- 1/4 cup all-purpose flour
- 1/2 teaspoon ground cinnamon
- 1/4 teaspoon ground nutmeg
- 1/4 teaspoon ground ginger
- 1/4 teaspoon ground cloves
- 1 teaspoon vanilla extract

For the Topping:

- 1 cup sour cream
- 2 tablespoons granulated sugar
- 1 teaspoon vanilla extract

Instructions:

1. Preheat the Oven:

- Preheat your oven to 325°F (163°C). Grease the bottom and sides of a 9-inch springform pan.

2. Prepare the Crust:

- In a bowl, combine graham cracker crumbs, melted butter, and sugar. Press the mixture into the bottom of the prepared springform pan to create a firm crust.

3. Bake the Crust:

    - Bake the crust in the preheated oven for about 10 minutes. Remove from the oven and let it cool while preparing the filling.

4. Prepare the Cheesecake Filling:

    - In a large mixing bowl, beat the softened cream cheese until smooth using an electric mixer.
    - Add sugar and beat until well combined.
    - Add eggs one at a time, beating well after each addition.
    - Mix in pumpkin puree, flour, cinnamon, nutmeg, ginger, cloves, and vanilla extract. Beat until the batter is smooth and well blended.

5. Pour Filling onto the Crust:

    - Pour the pumpkin-flavored cheesecake filling over the baked crust in the springform pan.

6. Bake the Cheesecake:

    - Bake in the preheated oven for about 1 hour or until the center is set and the top is lightly browned.

7. Prepare the Topping:

    - In a bowl, mix together sour cream, sugar, and vanilla extract for the topping.

8. Spread Topping:

    - Spread the sour cream topping over the baked cheesecake.

9. Bake Topping:

- Return the cheesecake to the oven and bake for an additional 10 minutes.

10. Cool and Refrigerate:

- Allow the cheesecake to cool in the pan on a wire rack. Once it reaches room temperature, cover and refrigerate for at least 4 hours or overnight.

11. Serve:

- Before serving, run a knife around the edge of the pan to loosen the cheesecake. Remove the sides of the springform pan.
- Slice and enjoy this delicious Pumpkin Cheesecake, perfect for fall and holiday celebrations!

This Pumpkin Cheesecake combines the warmth of pumpkin spices with the creaminess of cheesecake for a delightful and festive dessert.

Cherry Almond Cheesecake

Ingredients:

For the Crust:

- 1 1/2 cups almond meal
- 1/2 cup finely chopped almonds
- 1/4 cup melted unsalted butter
- 2 tablespoons granulated sugar

For the Cheesecake Filling:

- 4 packages (32 ounces) cream cheese, softened
- 1 1/4 cups granulated sugar
- 4 large eggs, room temperature
- 1/2 cup sour cream
- 1/2 cup heavy cream
- 1 teaspoon almond extract
- 1/2 cup all-purpose flour

For the Cherry Topping:

- 2 cups fresh or frozen cherries, pitted
- 1/2 cup granulated sugar
- 2 tablespoons water
- 1 tablespoon cornstarch
- 1 tablespoon lemon juice

For Garnish:

- Sliced almonds (toasted, optional)

Instructions:

1. Preheat the Oven:

- Preheat your oven to 325°F (163°C). Grease the bottom and sides of a 9-inch springform pan.

2. Prepare the Crust:

- In a bowl, mix almond meal, chopped almonds, melted butter, and sugar. Press the mixture into the bottom of the prepared springform pan to create a firm crust.

3. Bake the Crust:

- Bake the crust in the preheated oven for about 10 minutes. Remove from the oven and let it cool while preparing the filling.

4. Prepare the Cheesecake Filling:

- In a large mixing bowl, beat the softened cream cheese until smooth using an electric mixer.
- Add sugar and beat until well combined.
- Add eggs one at a time, beating well after each addition.
- Mix in sour cream, heavy cream, almond extract, and flour. Beat until the batter is smooth and well blended.

5. Pour Filling onto the Crust:

- Pour the almond-flavored cheesecake filling over the baked crust in the springform pan.

6. Bake the Cheesecake:

- Bake in the preheated oven for about 1 hour or until the center is set and the top is lightly browned.

7. Cool and Refrigerate:

- Allow the cheesecake to cool in the pan on a wire rack. Once it reaches room temperature, cover and refrigerate for at least 4 hours or overnight.

8. Prepare the Cherry Topping:

    - In a saucepan, combine cherries, sugar, water, cornstarch, and lemon juice. Cook over medium heat, stirring constantly until the mixture thickens and the cherries are soft.
    - Remove from heat and let the cherry topping cool.

9. Spread Cherry Topping:

    - Spread the cherry topping over the chilled cheesecake.

10. Garnish:

    - Garnish with toasted sliced almonds if desired.

11. Serve:

    - Before serving, run a knife around the edge of the pan to loosen the cheesecake. Remove the sides of the springform pan.
    - Slice and enjoy this luscious Cherry Almond Cheesecake, combining the flavors of sweet cherries and almond in a creamy delight!

Mint Chocolate Chip Cheesecake

Ingredients:

For the Crust:

- 2 cups chocolate cookie crumbs
- 1/2 cup melted unsalted butter
- 2 tablespoons granulated sugar

For the Cheesecake Filling:

- 4 packages (32 ounces) cream cheese, softened
- 1 1/4 cups granulated sugar
- 4 large eggs, room temperature
- 1 cup sour cream
- 1/4 cup all-purpose flour
- 1 teaspoon mint extract
- Green food coloring (optional)
- 1 cup mini chocolate chips

For the Chocolate Ganache:

- 1/2 cup heavy cream
- 1 cup semisweet chocolate chips
- 1/2 teaspoon mint extract

Instructions:

1. Preheat the Oven:

- Preheat your oven to 325°F (163°C). Grease the bottom and sides of a 9-inch springform pan.

2. Prepare the Crust:

- In a bowl, combine chocolate cookie crumbs, melted butter, and sugar. Press the mixture into the bottom of the prepared springform pan to create a firm crust.

3. Bake the Crust:

- Bake the crust in the preheated oven for about 10 minutes. Remove from the oven and let it cool while preparing the filling.

4. Prepare the Cheesecake Filling:

    - In a large mixing bowl, beat the softened cream cheese until smooth using an electric mixer.
    - Add sugar and beat until well combined.
    - Add eggs one at a time, beating well after each addition.
    - Mix in sour cream, flour, mint extract, and green food coloring (if using). Beat until the batter is smooth and well blended.
    - Fold in mini chocolate chips.

5. Pour Filling onto the Crust:

    - Pour the mint chocolate chip-flavored cheesecake filling over the baked crust in the springform pan.

6. Bake the Cheesecake:

    - Bake in the preheated oven for about 1 hour or until the center is set and the top is lightly browned.

7. Cool and Refrigerate:

    - Allow the cheesecake to cool in the pan on a wire rack. Once it reaches room temperature, cover and refrigerate for at least 4 hours or overnight.

8. Prepare the Chocolate Ganache:

    - In a saucepan, heat the heavy cream until it's just about to boil. Remove from heat and add chocolate chips and mint extract. Stir until smooth and well combined.

9. Pour Ganache over Cheesecake:

    - Pour the chocolate ganache over the chilled cheesecake, spreading it evenly.

10. Chill Again:

- Return the cheesecake to the refrigerator and let it chill until the ganache is set.

11. Serve:

    - Before serving, run a knife around the edge of the pan to loosen the cheesecake. Remove the sides of the springform pan.
    - Slice and savor this delightful Mint Chocolate Chip Cheesecake, featuring the refreshing flavor of mint and the richness of chocolate chips!

Pecan Pie Cheesecake

Ingredients:

For the Pecan Pie Layer:

- 1 cup chopped pecans
- 1/2 cup light corn syrup
- 1/4 cup granulated sugar
- 2 tablespoons unsalted butter, melted
- 1 teaspoon vanilla extract
- 3 large eggs, beaten

For the Cheesecake Layer:

For the Crust:

- 1 1/2 cups graham cracker crumbs
- 1/2 cup melted unsalted butter
- 2 tablespoons granulated sugar

For the Cheesecake Filling:

- 4 packages (32 ounces) cream cheese, softened
- 1 1/4 cups granulated sugar
- 4 large eggs, room temperature
- 1 cup sour cream
- 1/4 cup all-purpose flour
- 1 teaspoon vanilla extract

For Garnish:

- Additional chopped pecans, toasted

Instructions:

1. Preheat the Oven:

- Preheat your oven to 325°F (163°C). Grease the bottom and sides of a 9-inch springform pan.

2. Prepare the Pecan Pie Layer:

- In a bowl, combine chopped pecans, corn syrup, sugar, melted butter, vanilla extract, and beaten eggs. Mix well.

3. Prepare the Crust:

- In another bowl, mix graham cracker crumbs, melted butter, and sugar. Press the mixture into the bottom of the prepared springform pan to create a firm crust.

4. Spread Pecan Pie Layer:

- Spread the pecan pie mixture evenly over the crust.

5. Bake Pecan Pie Layer:

- Bake the pecan pie layer in the preheated oven for about 25-30 minutes or until set. Remove from the oven and let it cool.

6. Prepare the Cheesecake Filling:

- In a large mixing bowl, beat the softened cream cheese until smooth using an electric mixer.
- Add sugar and beat until well combined.
- Add eggs one at a time, beating well after each addition.
- Mix in sour cream, flour, and vanilla extract. Beat until the batter is smooth and well blended.

7. Assemble and Bake:

- Pour the cheesecake filling over the cooled pecan pie layer in the springform pan.
- Bake in the preheated oven for about 1 hour or until the center is set and the top is lightly browned.

8. Cool and Refrigerate:

- Allow the cheesecake to cool in the pan on a wire rack. Once it reaches room temperature, cover and refrigerate for at least 4 hours or overnight.

9. Garnish:

- Before serving, sprinkle additional chopped pecans over the top. You can toast them for added flavor.

10. Serve:

    - Before serving, run a knife around the edge of the pan to loosen the cheesecake. Remove the sides of the springform pan.
    - Slice and enjoy this decadent Pecan Pie Cheesecake, combining the best of both worlds with creamy cheesecake and pecan pie goodness!

Cookies and Cream Cheesecake

Ingredients:

For the Crust:

- 2 cups chocolate cookie crumbs (like Oreos)
- 1/2 cup melted unsalted butter

For the Cheesecake Filling:

- 4 packages (32 ounces) cream cheese, softened
- 1 1/4 cups granulated sugar
- 4 large eggs, room temperature
- 1 cup sour cream
- 1/4 cup all-purpose flour
- 1 teaspoon vanilla extract
- 1 1/2 cups crushed chocolate sandwich cookies (like Oreos)

For the Topping:

- 1 1/2 cups whipped cream
- Crushed chocolate sandwich cookies for garnish

Instructions:

1. Preheat the Oven:

- Preheat your oven to 325°F (163°C). Grease the bottom and sides of a 9-inch springform pan.

2. Prepare the Crust:

- In a bowl, mix chocolate cookie crumbs and melted butter. Press the mixture into the bottom of the prepared springform pan to create a firm crust.

3. Bake the Crust:

- Bake the crust in the preheated oven for about 10 minutes. Remove from the oven and let it cool while preparing the filling.

4. Prepare the Cheesecake Filling:

- In a large mixing bowl, beat the softened cream cheese until smooth using an electric mixer.
- Add sugar and vanilla extract, and beat until well combined.
- Add eggs one at a time, beating well after each addition.
- Mix in sour cream, flour, and crushed chocolate sandwich cookies. Beat until the batter is smooth and well blended.

5. Pour Filling onto the Crust:

- Pour the cookies and cream-flavored cheesecake filling over the baked crust in the springform pan.

6. Bake the Cheesecake:

- Bake in the preheated oven for about 1 hour or until the center is set and the top is lightly browned.

7. Cool and Refrigerate:

- Allow the cheesecake to cool in the pan on a wire rack. Once it reaches room temperature, cover and refrigerate for at least 4 hours or overnight.

8. Prepare the Topping:

- Before serving, spread whipped cream over the top of the chilled cheesecake.
- Garnish with additional crushed chocolate sandwich cookies.

9. Serve:

- Before serving, run a knife around the edge of the pan to loosen the cheesecake. Remove the sides of the springform pan.
- Slice and enjoy this Cookies and Cream Cheesecake, a delightful combination of creamy cheesecake and the classic flavor of chocolate sandwich cookies!

Red Velvet Cheesecake

Ingredients:

For the Red Velvet Crust:

- 1 1/2 cups red velvet cake crumbs (crumbled baked red velvet cake)
- 1/4 cup melted unsalted butter

For the Cheesecake Filling:

- 4 packages (32 ounces) cream cheese, softened
- 1 1/4 cups granulated sugar
- 4 large eggs, room temperature
- 1 cup sour cream
- 1/4 cup all-purpose flour
- 2 tablespoons unsweetened cocoa powder
- 1 teaspoon vanilla extract
- Red food coloring (as needed for a deeper red color)

For the Cream Cheese Frosting:

- 1/2 cup unsalted butter, softened
- 8 ounces cream cheese, softened
- 2 cups powdered sugar
- 1 teaspoon vanilla extract

Instructions:

1. Preheat the Oven:

- Preheat your oven to 325°F (163°C). Grease the bottom and sides of a 9-inch springform pan.

2. Prepare the Red Velvet Crust:

- In a bowl, mix red velvet cake crumbs and melted butter. Press the mixture into the bottom of the prepared springform pan to create a firm crust.

3. Prepare the Cheesecake Filling:

    - In a large mixing bowl, beat the softened cream cheese until smooth using an electric mixer.
    - Add sugar and vanilla extract, and beat until well combined.
    - Add eggs one at a time, beating well after each addition.
    - Mix in sour cream, flour, cocoa powder, and red food coloring. Beat until the batter is smooth and well blended. Adjust the amount of food coloring for the desired color.

4. Pour Filling onto the Crust:

    - Pour the red velvet-flavored cheesecake filling over the red velvet crust in the springform pan.

5. Bake the Cheesecake:

    - Bake in the preheated oven for about 1 hour or until the center is set and the top is lightly browned.

6. Cool and Refrigerate:

    - Allow the cheesecake to cool in the pan on a wire rack. Once it reaches room temperature, cover and refrigerate for at least 4 hours or overnight.

7. Prepare the Cream Cheese Frosting:

    - In a bowl, beat together softened butter, cream cheese, powdered sugar, and vanilla extract until smooth and creamy.

8. Frost the Cheesecake:

    - Once the cheesecake is thoroughly chilled, spread a layer of cream cheese frosting over the top.

9. Serve:

- Before serving, run a knife around the edge of the pan to loosen the cheesecake. Remove the sides of the springform pan.
- Slice and enjoy this Red Velvet Cheesecake, combining the luscious flavors of red velvet cake and creamy cheesecake, topped with a layer of decadent cream cheese frosting!

Mocha Cheesecake

Ingredients:

For the Crust:

- 2 cups chocolate cookie crumbs
- 1/2 cup melted unsalted butter
- 2 tablespoons granulated sugar

For the Cheesecake Filling:

- 4 packages (32 ounces) cream cheese, softened
- 1 1/4 cups granulated sugar
- 4 large eggs, room temperature
- 1 cup sour cream
- 1/4 cup all-purpose flour
- 1 teaspoon vanilla extract
- 2 tablespoons instant coffee or espresso powder, dissolved in 2 tablespoons hot water
- 1/2 cup chocolate chips or chunks

For the Mocha Ganache:

- 1/2 cup heavy cream
- 1 cup semisweet chocolate chips
- 1 tablespoon instant coffee or espresso powder

Instructions:

1. Preheat the Oven:

- Preheat your oven to 325°F (163°C). Grease the bottom and sides of a 9-inch springform pan.

2. Prepare the Crust:

- In a bowl, mix chocolate cookie crumbs, melted butter, and sugar. Press the mixture into the bottom of the prepared springform pan to create a firm crust.

3. Bake the Crust:

    - Bake the crust in the preheated oven for about 10 minutes. Remove from the oven and let it cool while preparing the filling.

4. Prepare the Cheesecake Filling:

    - In a large mixing bowl, beat the softened cream cheese until smooth using an electric mixer.
    - Add sugar and vanilla extract, and beat until well combined.
    - Add eggs one at a time, beating well after each addition.
    - Mix in sour cream, flour, and the dissolved instant coffee or espresso. Beat until the batter is smooth and well blended.
    - Fold in chocolate chips or chunks.

5. Pour Filling onto the Crust:

    - Pour the mocha-flavored cheesecake filling over the baked crust in the springform pan.

6. Bake the Cheesecake:

    - Bake in the preheated oven for about 1 hour or until the center is set and the top is lightly browned.

7. Cool and Refrigerate:

    - Allow the cheesecake to cool in the pan on a wire rack. Once it reaches room temperature, cover and refrigerate for at least 4 hours or overnight.

8. Prepare the Mocha Ganache:

- In a saucepan, heat the heavy cream until it's just about to boil. Remove from heat and add chocolate chips and instant coffee or espresso powder. Stir until smooth and well combined.

9. Pour Ganache over Cheesecake:

- Pour the mocha ganache over the chilled cheesecake, spreading it evenly.

10. Chill Again:

- Return the cheesecake to the refrigerator and let it chill until the ganache is set.

11. Serve:

- Before serving, run a knife around the edge of the pan to loosen the cheesecake. Remove the sides of the springform pan.
- Slice and enjoy this Mocha Cheesecake, featuring the rich flavors of coffee and chocolate in a creamy, decadent dessert!

Maple Pecan Cheesecake

Ingredients:

For the Pecan Crust:

- 1 1/2 cups pecan halves
- 1/4 cup granulated sugar
- 1/4 cup melted unsalted butter

For the Cheesecake Filling:

- 4 packages (32 ounces) cream cheese, softened
- 1 cup pure maple syrup
- 1/2 cup granulated sugar
- 4 large eggs, room temperature
- 1/2 cup sour cream
- 1/4 cup all-purpose flour
- 1 teaspoon vanilla extract

For the Maple Pecan Topping:

- 1 cup pecan halves, toasted
- 1/4 cup pure maple syrup

Instructions:

1. Preheat the Oven:

- Preheat your oven to 325°F (163°C). Grease the bottom and sides of a 9-inch springform pan.

2. Prepare the Pecan Crust:

- In a food processor, pulse pecan halves and sugar until finely ground. Add melted butter and pulse until well combined.

- Press the pecan mixture into the bottom of the prepared springform pan to create a firm crust.

3. Bake the Crust:

- Bake the crust in the preheated oven for about 10 minutes. Remove from the oven and let it cool while preparing the filling.

4. Prepare the Cheesecake Filling:

- In a large mixing bowl, beat the softened cream cheese until smooth using an electric mixer.
- Add maple syrup, sugar, and vanilla extract. Beat until well combined.
- Add eggs one at a time, beating well after each addition.
- Mix in sour cream and flour. Beat until the batter is smooth and well blended.

5. Pour Filling onto the Crust:

- Pour the maple pecan-flavored cheesecake filling over the baked crust in the springform pan.

6. Bake the Cheesecake:

- Bake in the preheated oven for about 1 hour or until the center is set and the top is lightly browned.

7. Cool and Refrigerate:

- Allow the cheesecake to cool in the pan on a wire rack. Once it reaches room temperature, cover and refrigerate for at least 4 hours or overnight.

8. Prepare the Maple Pecan Topping:

- Toast pecan halves in a dry skillet over medium heat until fragrant. Add pure maple syrup and continue toasting until the pecans are coated and the syrup thickens slightly.

9. Top the Cheesecake:

- Spread the maple pecan topping over the chilled cheesecake, ensuring an even distribution.

10. Serve:

- Before serving, run a knife around the edge of the pan to loosen the cheesecake. Remove the sides of the springform pan.
- Slice and savor this Maple Pecan Cheesecake, combining the warmth of maple and the crunch of pecans in a creamy and indulgent dessert!

Banana Foster Cheesecake

Ingredients:

For the Crust:

- 2 cups graham cracker crumbs
- 1/2 cup melted unsalted butter
- 2 tablespoons granulated sugar

For the Cheesecake Filling:

- 4 packages (32 ounces) cream cheese, softened
- 1 cup granulated sugar
- 4 large eggs, room temperature
- 1 cup mashed ripe bananas (about 2-3 bananas)
- 1/4 cup all-purpose flour
- 1 teaspoon vanilla extract
- 1/4 cup dark rum (for an authentic Banana Foster flavor)

For the Banana Foster Topping:

- 1/4 cup unsalted butter
- 1/2 cup packed brown sugar
- 1/4 cup dark rum
- 4 ripe bananas, sliced
- 1 teaspoon vanilla extract
- Whipped cream and sliced bananas for garnish

Instructions:

1. Preheat the Oven:

- Preheat your oven to 325°F (163°C). Grease the bottom and sides of a 9-inch springform pan.

2. Prepare the Crust:

- In a bowl, mix graham cracker crumbs, melted butter, and sugar. Press the mixture into the bottom of the prepared springform pan to create a firm crust.

3. Bake the Crust:

    - Bake the crust in the preheated oven for about 10 minutes. Remove from the oven and let it cool while preparing the filling.

4. Prepare the Cheesecake Filling:

    - In a large mixing bowl, beat the softened cream cheese until smooth using an electric mixer.
    - Add sugar, mashed bananas, vanilla extract, and dark rum. Beat until well combined.
    - Add eggs one at a time, beating well after each addition.
    - Mix in flour and beat until the batter is smooth and well blended.

5. Pour Filling onto the Crust:

    - Pour the banana foster-flavored cheesecake filling over the baked crust in the springform pan.

6. Bake the Cheesecake:

    - Bake in the preheated oven for about 1 hour or until the center is set and the top is lightly browned.

7. Cool and Refrigerate:

    - Allow the cheesecake to cool in the pan on a wire rack. Once it reaches room temperature, cover and refrigerate for at least 4 hours or overnight.

8. Prepare the Banana Foster Topping:

    - In a skillet, melt butter over medium heat. Add brown sugar, dark rum, sliced bananas, and vanilla extract.
    - Cook, stirring gently, until the bananas are caramelized and the sauce thickens.

9. Top the Cheesecake:

- Spread the banana foster topping over the chilled cheesecake, ensuring an even distribution.

10. Garnish and Serve:

- Before serving, garnish with whipped cream and additional sliced bananas if desired.
- Slice and indulge in this Banana Foster Cheesecake, a delightful combination of creamy cheesecake and the rich, caramelized flavors of banana foster!

Pistachio Cheesecake

Ingredients:

For the Pistachio Crust:

- 1 1/2 cups shelled pistachios
- 1/4 cup granulated sugar
- 1/4 cup melted unsalted butter

For the Cheesecake Filling:

- 4 packages (32 ounces) cream cheese, softened
- 1 cup granulated sugar
- 4 large eggs, room temperature
- 1 cup sour cream
- 1/4 cup all-purpose flour
- 1 teaspoon vanilla extract
- 1 cup pistachio paste or ground pistachios

For the Pistachio Topping:

- 1 cup shelled pistachios, chopped
- 1/4 cup powdered sugar (for dusting)

Instructions:

1. Preheat the Oven:

- Preheat your oven to 325°F (163°C). Grease the bottom and sides of a 9-inch springform pan.

2. Prepare the Pistachio Crust:

- In a food processor, pulse shelled pistachios until finely ground. Add sugar and melted butter, and pulse until well combined.

- Press the pistachio mixture into the bottom of the prepared springform pan to create a firm crust.

3. Bake the Crust:

    - Bake the crust in the preheated oven for about 10 minutes. Remove from the oven and let it cool while preparing the filling.

4. Prepare the Cheesecake Filling:

    - In a large mixing bowl, beat the softened cream cheese until smooth using an electric mixer.
    - Add sugar, vanilla extract, and pistachio paste or ground pistachios. Beat until well combined.
    - Add eggs one at a time, beating well after each addition.
    - Mix in sour cream and flour. Beat until the batter is smooth and well blended.

5. Pour Filling onto the Crust:

    - Pour the pistachio-flavored cheesecake filling over the baked crust in the springform pan.

6. Bake the Cheesecake:

    - Bake in the preheated oven for about 1 hour or until the center is set and the top is lightly browned.

7. Cool and Refrigerate:

    - Allow the cheesecake to cool in the pan on a wire rack. Once it reaches room temperature, cover and refrigerate for at least 4 hours or overnight.

8. Prepare the Pistachio Topping:

    - Before serving, top the cheesecake with chopped pistachios and dust with powdered sugar.

9. Serve:

- Before serving, run a knife around the edge of the pan to loosen the cheesecake. Remove the sides of the springform pan.
- Slice and enjoy this Pistachio Cheesecake, featuring the nutty flavor of pistachios in a creamy and decadent dessert!

Coconut Lime Cheesecake

Ingredients:

For the Crust:

- 2 cups graham cracker crumbs
- 1/2 cup melted unsalted butter
- 2 tablespoons granulated sugar

For the Cheesecake Filling:

- 4 packages (32 ounces) cream cheese, softened
- 1 cup granulated sugar
- 4 large eggs, room temperature
- 1 cup coconut cream
- Zest of 2 limes
- 1/4 cup lime juice
- 1/4 cup all-purpose flour
- 1 teaspoon vanilla extract

For the Coconut Lime Topping:

- 1 cup shredded coconut, toasted
- Zest of 1 lime
- 2 tablespoons lime juice
- 2 tablespoons powdered sugar (optional, for sweetness)

Instructions:

1. Preheat the Oven:

- Preheat your oven to 325°F (163°C). Grease the bottom and sides of a 9-inch springform pan.

2. Prepare the Crust:

- In a bowl, mix graham cracker crumbs, melted butter, and sugar. Press the mixture into the bottom of the prepared springform pan to create a firm crust.

3. Bake the Crust:

    - Bake the crust in the preheated oven for about 10 minutes. Remove from the oven and let it cool while preparing the filling.

4. Prepare the Cheesecake Filling:

    - In a large mixing bowl, beat the softened cream cheese until smooth using an electric mixer.
    - Add sugar, lime zest, lime juice, coconut cream, and vanilla extract. Beat until well combined.
    - Add eggs one at a time, beating well after each addition.
    - Mix in flour and beat until the batter is smooth and well blended.

5. Pour Filling onto the Crust:

    - Pour the coconut lime-flavored cheesecake filling over the baked crust in the springform pan.

6. Bake the Cheesecake:

    - Bake in the preheated oven for about 1 hour or until the center is set and the top is lightly browned.

7. Cool and Refrigerate:

    - Allow the cheesecake to cool in the pan on a wire rack. Once it reaches room temperature, cover and refrigerate for at least 4 hours or overnight.

8. Prepare the Coconut Lime Topping:

    - In a bowl, combine toasted shredded coconut, lime zest, lime juice, and powdered sugar (if using). Mix well.

9. Top the Cheesecake:

- Spread the coconut lime topping over the chilled cheesecake, ensuring an even distribution.

10. Serve:

- Before serving, run a knife around the edge of the pan to loosen the cheesecake. Remove the sides of the springform pan.
- Slice and enjoy this Coconut Lime Cheesecake, a refreshing and tropical twist on the classic dessert!

White Chocolate Raspberry Cheesecake

Ingredients:

For the Crust:

- 2 cups graham cracker crumbs
- 1/2 cup melted unsalted butter
- 2 tablespoons granulated sugar

For the White Chocolate Raspberry Cheesecake Filling:

- 4 packages (32 ounces) cream cheese, softened
- 1 1/4 cups granulated sugar
- 4 large eggs, room temperature
- 1 cup white chocolate chips, melted and cooled slightly
- 1/4 cup all-purpose flour
- 1 teaspoon vanilla extract
- 1 cup fresh raspberries

For the Raspberry Sauce:

- 1 cup fresh or frozen raspberries
- 2 tablespoons granulated sugar
- 1 tablespoon water
- 1 teaspoon lemon juice (optional)

Instructions:

1. Preheat the Oven:

- Preheat your oven to 325°F (163°C). Grease the bottom and sides of a 9-inch springform pan.

2. Prepare the Crust:

- In a bowl, mix graham cracker crumbs, melted butter, and sugar. Press the mixture into the bottom of the prepared springform pan to create a firm crust.

3. Bake the Crust:

- Bake the crust in the preheated oven for about 10 minutes. Remove from the oven and let it cool while preparing the filling.

4. Prepare the Cheesecake Filling:

- In a large mixing bowl, beat the softened cream cheese until smooth using an electric mixer.
- Add sugar and vanilla extract. Beat until well combined.
- Add eggs one at a time, beating well after each addition.
- Mix in melted white chocolate and flour. Beat until the batter is smooth and well blended.
- Gently fold in fresh raspberries.

5. Pour Filling onto the Crust:

- Pour the white chocolate raspberry-flavored cheesecake filling over the baked crust in the springform pan.

6. Bake the Cheesecake:

- Bake in the preheated oven for about 1 hour or until the center is set and the top is lightly browned.

7. Cool and Refrigerate:

- Allow the cheesecake to cool in the pan on a wire rack. Once it reaches room temperature, cover and refrigerate for at least 4 hours or overnight.

8. Prepare the Raspberry Sauce:

- In a saucepan, combine raspberries, sugar, water, and lemon juice (if using). Cook over medium heat, stirring occasionally, until the raspberries break down and the sauce thickens. Strain to remove seeds if desired.

9. Top the Cheesecake:

- Drizzle the raspberry sauce over the chilled cheesecake before serving.

10. Serve:

- Before serving, run a knife around the edge of the pan to loosen the cheesecake. Remove the sides of the springform pan.
- Slice and enjoy this White Chocolate Raspberry Cheesecake, a perfect blend of creamy, sweet white chocolate and tart raspberries!

Espresso Cheesecake

Ingredients:

For the Espresso Crust:

- 2 cups chocolate cookie crumbs
- 1/2 cup melted unsalted butter
- 2 tablespoons granulated sugar
- 2 tablespoons finely ground espresso beans

For the Cheesecake Filling:

- 4 packages (32 ounces) cream cheese, softened
- 1 1/4 cups granulated sugar
- 4 large eggs, room temperature
- 1/4 cup all-purpose flour
- 1 teaspoon vanilla extract
- 1/4 cup strong brewed espresso, cooled

For the Espresso Ganache:

- 1/2 cup heavy cream
- 1 cup semisweet chocolate chips
- 1 tablespoon finely ground espresso beans

Instructions:

1. Preheat the Oven:

- Preheat your oven to 325°F (163°C). Grease the bottom and sides of a 9-inch springform pan.

2. Prepare the Espresso Crust:

- In a bowl, mix chocolate cookie crumbs, melted butter, sugar, and finely ground espresso beans. Press the mixture into the bottom of the prepared springform pan to create a firm crust.

3. Bake the Crust:

- Bake the crust in the preheated oven for about 10 minutes. Remove from the oven and let it cool while preparing the filling.

4. Prepare the Cheesecake Filling:

- In a large mixing bowl, beat the softened cream cheese until smooth using an electric mixer.
- Add sugar, vanilla extract, and flour. Beat until well combined.
- Add eggs one at a time, beating well after each addition.
- Mix in the cooled brewed espresso. Beat until the batter is smooth and well blended.

5. Pour Filling onto the Crust:

- Pour the espresso-flavored cheesecake filling over the baked crust in the springform pan.

6. Bake the Cheesecake:

- Bake in the preheated oven for about 1 hour or until the center is set and the top is lightly browned.

7. Cool and Refrigerate:

- Allow the cheesecake to cool in the pan on a wire rack. Once it reaches room temperature, cover and refrigerate for at least 4 hours or overnight.

8. Prepare the Espresso Ganache:

- In a saucepan, heat the heavy cream until it's just about to boil. Remove from heat and add chocolate chips and finely ground espresso beans. Stir until smooth and well combined.

9. Pour Ganache over Cheesecake:

- Pour the espresso ganache over the chilled cheesecake, spreading it evenly.

10. Chill Again:

- Return the cheesecake to the refrigerator and let it chill until the ganache is set.

11. Serve:

- Before serving, run a knife around the edge of the pan to loosen the cheesecake. Remove the sides of the springform pan.
- Slice and savor this Espresso Cheesecake, featuring the rich and bold flavors of espresso in a creamy and indulgent dessert!

Strawberry Shortcake Cheesecake

Ingredients:

For the Shortcake Crust:

- 2 cups shortbread cookie crumbs
- 1/2 cup melted unsalted butter
- 2 tablespoons granulated sugar

For the Cheesecake Filling:

- 4 packages (32 ounces) cream cheese, softened
- 1 cup granulated sugar
- 4 large eggs, room temperature
- 1/4 cup all-purpose flour
- 1 teaspoon vanilla extract
- 1/4 cup heavy cream

For the Strawberry Topping:

- 2 cups fresh strawberries, hulled and sliced
- 1/4 cup granulated sugar
- 1 tablespoon lemon juice

For the Whipped Cream:

- 1 cup heavy cream
- 2 tablespoons powdered sugar
- 1 teaspoon vanilla extract

Instructions:

1. Preheat the Oven:

- Preheat your oven to 325°F (163°C). Grease the bottom and sides of a 9-inch springform pan.

2. Prepare the Shortcake Crust:

   - In a bowl, mix shortbread cookie crumbs, melted butter, and sugar. Press the mixture into the bottom of the prepared springform pan to create a firm crust.

3. Bake the Crust:

   - Bake the crust in the preheated oven for about 10 minutes. Remove from the oven and let it cool while preparing the filling.

4. Prepare the Cheesecake Filling:

   - In a large mixing bowl, beat the softened cream cheese until smooth using an electric mixer.
   - Add sugar, vanilla extract, and flour. Beat until well combined.
   - Add eggs one at a time, beating well after each addition.
   - Mix in heavy cream and beat until the batter is smooth and well blended.

5. Pour Filling onto the Crust:

   - Pour the cheesecake filling over the baked shortcake crust in the springform pan.

6. Bake the Cheesecake:

   - Bake in the preheated oven for about 1 hour or until the center is set and the top is lightly browned.

7. Cool and Refrigerate:

   - Allow the cheesecake to cool in the pan on a wire rack. Once it reaches room temperature, cover and refrigerate for at least 4 hours or overnight.

8. Prepare the Strawberry Topping:

- In a bowl, combine sliced strawberries, sugar, and lemon juice. Let it sit for about 15-20 minutes to allow the strawberries to release their juices.

9. Make Whipped Cream:

- In a separate bowl, whip the heavy cream, powdered sugar, and vanilla extract until stiff peaks form.

10. Assemble the Cheesecake:

- Just before serving, spread the macerated strawberries over the chilled cheesecake.
- Dollop whipped cream on top and around the edges.

11. Serve:

- Before serving, run a knife around the edge of the pan to loosen the cheesecake. Remove the sides of the springform pan.
- Slice and enjoy this Strawberry Shortcake Cheesecake, a luscious combination of creamy cheesecake, buttery shortcake crust, and fresh strawberries with a touch of whipped cream!

Almond Joy Cheesecake

Ingredients:

For the Almond Joy Crust:

- 2 cups chocolate cookie crumbs
- 1/2 cup melted unsalted butter
- 1/4 cup shredded coconut
- 1/4 cup chopped almonds

For the Cheesecake Filling:

- 4 packages (32 ounces) cream cheese, softened
- 1 cup granulated sugar
- 4 large eggs, room temperature
- 1/4 cup all-purpose flour
- 1 teaspoon vanilla extract
- 1/2 cup shredded coconut
- 1/2 cup chopped almonds
- 1/2 cup chocolate chips (milk or dark)

For the Chocolate Ganache:

- 1/2 cup heavy cream
- 1 cup semisweet chocolate chips

For the Toppings:

- Additional shredded coconut, chopped almonds, and chocolate chips for garnish

Instructions:

1. Preheat the Oven:

- Preheat your oven to 325°F (163°C). Grease the bottom and sides of a 9-inch springform pan.

2. Prepare the Almond Joy Crust:

   - In a bowl, mix chocolate cookie crumbs, melted butter, shredded coconut, and chopped almonds. Press the mixture into the bottom of the prepared springform pan to create a firm crust.

3. Bake the Crust:

   - Bake the crust in the preheated oven for about 10 minutes. Remove from the oven and let it cool while preparing the filling.

4. Prepare the Cheesecake Filling:

   - In a large mixing bowl, beat the softened cream cheese until smooth using an electric mixer.
   - Add sugar, vanilla extract, and flour. Beat until well combined.
   - Add eggs one at a time, beating well after each addition.
   - Mix in shredded coconut, chopped almonds, and chocolate chips. Beat until the batter is smooth and well blended.

5. Pour Filling onto the Crust:

   - Pour the Almond Joy-flavored cheesecake filling over the baked crust in the springform pan.

6. Bake the Cheesecake:

   - Bake in the preheated oven for about 1 hour or until the center is set and the top is lightly browned.

7. Cool and Refrigerate:

   - Allow the cheesecake to cool in the pan on a wire rack. Once it reaches room temperature, cover and refrigerate for at least 4 hours or overnight.

8. Prepare the Chocolate Ganache:

   - In a saucepan, heat the heavy cream until it's just about to boil. Remove from heat and add chocolate chips. Stir until smooth and well combined.

9. Pour Ganache over Cheesecake:

   - Pour the chocolate ganache over the chilled cheesecake, spreading it evenly.

10. Decorate with Toppings:

    - Sprinkle additional shredded coconut, chopped almonds, and chocolate chips over the chocolate ganache while it's still soft.

11. Chill Again:

    - Return the cheesecake to the refrigerator and let it chill until the ganache is set.

12. Serve:

    - Before serving, run a knife around the edge of the pan to loosen the cheesecake. Remove the sides of the springform pan.
    - Slice and enjoy this Almond Joy Cheesecake, a delightful blend of coconut, almonds, and chocolate in a creamy cheesecake form!

Black Forest Cheesecake

Ingredients:

For the Chocolate Crust:

- 2 cups chocolate cookie crumbs
- 1/2 cup melted unsalted butter
- 2 tablespoons granulated sugar

For the Cheesecake Filling:

- 4 packages (32 ounces) cream cheese, softened
- 1 cup granulated sugar
- 4 large eggs, room temperature
- 1/4 cup all-purpose flour
- 1 teaspoon vanilla extract
- 1/4 cup cocoa powder
- 1/4 cup strong brewed coffee, cooled

For the Cherry Topping:

- 2 cups fresh or canned cherries, pitted and halved
- 1/2 cup granulated sugar
- 1 tablespoon cornstarch
- 1 tablespoon lemon juice

For Whipped Cream:

- 1 cup heavy cream
- 2 tablespoons powdered sugar
- 1 teaspoon vanilla extract

For Chocolate Shavings (Optional):

- Dark chocolate bar

Instructions:

1. Preheat the Oven:

- Preheat your oven to 325°F (163°C). Grease the bottom and sides of a 9-inch springform pan.

2. Prepare the Chocolate Crust:

    - In a bowl, mix chocolate cookie crumbs, melted butter, and sugar. Press the mixture into the bottom of the prepared springform pan to create a firm crust.

3. Bake the Crust:

    - Bake the crust in the preheated oven for about 10 minutes. Remove from the oven and let it cool while preparing the filling.

4. Prepare the Cheesecake Filling:

    - In a large mixing bowl, beat the softened cream cheese until smooth using an electric mixer.
    - Add sugar, vanilla extract, and flour. Beat until well combined.
    - Add eggs one at a time, beating well after each addition.
    - Mix in cocoa powder and brewed coffee. Beat until the batter is smooth and well blended.

5. Pour Filling onto the Crust:

    - Pour the chocolate-flavored cheesecake filling over the baked crust in the springform pan.

6. Bake the Cheesecake:

    - Bake in the preheated oven for about 1 hour or until the center is set and the top is lightly browned.

7. Cool and Refrigerate:

    - Allow the cheesecake to cool in the pan on a wire rack. Once it reaches room temperature, cover and refrigerate for at least 4 hours or overnight.

8. Prepare the Cherry Topping:

- In a saucepan, combine cherries, sugar, cornstarch, and lemon juice. Cook over medium heat until the mixture thickens and the cherries release their juices. Let it cool.

9. Make Whipped Cream:

    - In a separate bowl, whip the heavy cream, powdered sugar, and vanilla extract until stiff peaks form.

10. Assemble the Cheesecake:

    - Spread the cherry topping over the chilled cheesecake.
    - Dollop whipped cream on top and around the edges.

11. Optional: Add Chocolate Shavings:

    - Use a vegetable peeler to create chocolate shavings from a dark chocolate bar. Sprinkle the shavings over the whipped cream.

12. Serve:

    - Before serving, run a knife around the edge of the pan to loosen the cheesecake. Remove the sides of the springform pan.
    - Slice and enjoy this Black Forest Cheesecake, a delightful combination of rich chocolate, creamy cheesecake, and sweet cherries!

Caramel Apple Cheesecake

Ingredients:

For the Apple Crisp Topping:

- 2 cups finely chopped apples (peeled and cored)
- 2 tablespoons unsalted butter
- 2 tablespoons brown sugar
- 1/2 teaspoon ground cinnamon
- 1/4 teaspoon nutmeg

For the Caramel Sauce:

- 1 cup granulated sugar
- 6 tablespoons unsalted butter
- 1/2 cup heavy cream
- 1 teaspoon vanilla extract
- 1/4 teaspoon salt

For the Cheesecake Filling:

- 2 cups graham cracker crumbs
- 1/2 cup melted unsalted butter
- 4 packages (32 ounces) cream cheese, softened
- 1 cup granulated sugar
- 4 large eggs, room temperature
- 1/4 cup all-purpose flour
- 1 teaspoon vanilla extract

For Garnish:

- Additional caramel sauce
- Chopped nuts (optional)

Instructions:

1. Preheat the Oven:

   - Preheat your oven to 325°F (163°C). Grease the bottom and sides of a 9-inch springform pan.

2. Prepare the Apple Crisp Topping:

   - In a skillet, melt 2 tablespoons of butter over medium heat. Add chopped apples, brown sugar, ground cinnamon, and nutmeg. Cook until the apples are soft and caramelized. Set aside to cool.

3. Make the Caramel Sauce:

   - In a saucepan over medium heat, melt granulated sugar, stirring continuously until it turns into a smooth amber-colored liquid.
   - Add butter and stir until melted.
   - Slowly pour in heavy cream while stirring continuously. Be cautious as the mixture will bubble.
   - Continue stirring until the caramel sauce is smooth. Remove from heat and stir in vanilla extract and salt. Set aside to cool.

4. Prepare the Cheesecake Crust:

   - In a bowl, mix graham cracker crumbs and melted butter. Press the mixture into the bottom of the prepared springform pan to create a firm crust.

5. Prepare the Cheesecake Filling:

   - In a large mixing bowl, beat the softened cream cheese until smooth using an electric mixer.
   - Add sugar, vanilla extract, and flour. Beat until well combined.
   - Add eggs one at a time, beating well after each addition.

6. Assemble the Cheesecake:

   - Pour half of the cheesecake batter over the crust in the springform pan.
   - Spoon half of the caramel sauce over the batter and swirl it with a knife.

- Add the remaining cheesecake batter and top with the apple crisp topping.
- Drizzle the remaining caramel sauce over the top.

7. Bake the Cheesecake:

- Bake in the preheated oven for about 1 hour or until the center is set and the top is lightly browned.

8. Cool and Refrigerate:

- Allow the cheesecake to cool in the pan on a wire rack. Once it reaches room temperature, cover and refrigerate for at least 4 hours or overnight.

9. Garnish:

- Before serving, drizzle additional caramel sauce over the top and sprinkle chopped nuts if desired.

10. Serve:

- Before serving, run a knife around the edge of the pan to loosen the cheesecake. Remove the sides of the springform pan.
- Slice and indulge in this Caramel Apple Cheesecake, a heavenly combination of creamy cheesecake, caramel sauce, and apple crisp topping!

Chocolate Hazelnut Cheesecake

Ingredients:

For the Hazelnut Crust:

- 2 cups hazelnuts, toasted and finely ground
- 1/4 cup sugar
- 1/2 cup unsalted butter, melted

For the Chocolate Hazelnut Filling:

- 4 packages (32 ounces) cream cheese, softened
- 1 cup sugar
- 4 large eggs, room temperature
- 1 teaspoon vanilla extract
- 1 cup chocolate hazelnut spread (like Nutella)
- 1/4 cup all-purpose flour
- 1/2 cup heavy cream

For the Hazelnut Ganache:

- 1/2 cup hazelnuts, chopped and toasted
- 1/2 cup heavy cream
- 1 cup semisweet chocolate chips

Instructions:

1. Preheat the Oven:

- Preheat your oven to 325°F (163°C). Grease the bottom and sides of a 9-inch springform pan.

2. Prepare the Hazelnut Crust:

- In a bowl, combine finely ground toasted hazelnuts, sugar, and melted butter. Press the mixture into the bottom of the prepared springform pan to create a firm crust.

3. Bake the Crust:

    - Bake the crust in the preheated oven for about 10 minutes. Remove from the oven and let it cool while preparing the filling.

4. Prepare the Chocolate Hazelnut Filling:

    - In a large mixing bowl, beat the softened cream cheese until smooth using an electric mixer.
    - Add sugar, vanilla extract, and chocolate hazelnut spread. Beat until well combined.
    - Add eggs one at a time, beating well after each addition.
    - Mix in flour and heavy cream. Beat until the batter is smooth and well blended.

5. Pour Filling onto the Crust:

    - Pour the chocolate hazelnut-flavored cheesecake filling over the baked hazelnut crust in the springform pan.

6. Bake the Cheesecake:

    - Bake in the preheated oven for about 1 hour or until the center is set and the top is lightly browned.

7. Cool and Refrigerate:

    - Allow the cheesecake to cool in the pan on a wire rack. Once it reaches room temperature, cover and refrigerate for at least 4 hours or overnight.

8. Prepare the Hazelnut Ganache:

    - In a saucepan, heat the heavy cream until it's just about to boil. Remove from heat and add chocolate chips. Stir until smooth and well combined.

9. Pour Ganache over Cheesecake:

- Pour the hazelnut ganache over the chilled cheesecake, spreading it evenly.

10. Sprinkle Chopped Hazelnuts:

- Sprinkle chopped and toasted hazelnuts over the ganache while it's still soft.

11. Chill Again:

- Return the cheesecake to the refrigerator and let it chill until the ganache is set.

12. Serve:

- Before serving, run a knife around the edge of the pan to loosen the cheesecake. Remove the sides of the springform pan.
- Slice and enjoy this Chocolate Hazelnut Cheesecake, a decadent treat for hazelnut and chocolate lovers!

Mango Passionfruit Cheesecake

Ingredients:

For the Mango Passionfruit Puree:

- 2 ripe mangoes, peeled and diced
- Pulp from 4 passionfruits
- 2 tablespoons sugar (adjust according to sweetness)

For the Cheesecake Filling:

- 4 packages (32 ounces) cream cheese, softened
- 1 cup sugar
- 4 large eggs, room temperature
- 1 teaspoon vanilla extract
- 1/2 cup sour cream
- 1/2 cup mango passionfruit puree

For the Crust:

- 2 cups graham cracker crumbs
- 1/2 cup melted unsalted butter
- 2 tablespoons sugar

For Garnish:

- Fresh mango slices
- Passionfruit seeds

Instructions:

1. Preheat the Oven:

- Preheat your oven to 325°F (163°C). Grease the bottom and sides of a 9-inch springform pan.

2. Prepare the Crust:

- In a bowl, mix graham cracker crumbs, melted butter, and sugar. Press the mixture into the bottom of the prepared springform pan to create a firm crust.

3. Bake the Crust:

    - Bake the crust in the preheated oven for about 10 minutes. Remove from the oven and let it cool while preparing the filling.

4. Prepare the Mango Passionfruit Puree:

    - In a blender or food processor, blend the diced mangoes, passionfruit pulp, and sugar until smooth. Set aside.

5. Prepare the Cheesecake Filling:

    - In a large mixing bowl, beat the softened cream cheese until smooth using an electric mixer.
    - Add sugar, vanilla extract, and eggs one at a time, beating well after each addition.
    - Mix in sour cream and mango passionfruit puree. Beat until the batter is smooth and well blended.

6. Pour Filling onto the Crust:

    - Pour the mango passionfruit-flavored cheesecake filling over the baked crust in the springform pan.

7. Bake the Cheesecake:

    - Bake in the preheated oven for about 1 hour or until the center is set and the top is lightly browned.

8. Cool and Refrigerate:

    - Allow the cheesecake to cool in the pan on a wire rack. Once it reaches room temperature, cover and refrigerate for at least 4 hours or overnight.

9. Garnish:

- Before serving, garnish the cheesecake with fresh mango slices and passionfruit seeds.

10. Serve:

- Before serving, run a knife around the edge of the pan to loosen the cheesecake. Remove the sides of the springform pan.
- Slice and savor this Mango Passionfruit Cheesecake, a tropical delight perfect for a refreshing dessert!

S'mores Cheesecake

Ingredients:

For the Crust:

- 2 cups graham cracker crumbs
- 1/2 cup melted unsalted butter
- 2 tablespoons sugar

For the Cheesecake Filling:

- 4 packages (32 ounces) cream cheese, softened
- 1 cup sugar
- 4 large eggs, room temperature
- 1 teaspoon vanilla extract
- 1/2 cup sour cream
- 1/2 cup chocolate chips

For the Topping:

- 1 cup mini marshmallows
- 1/2 cup chocolate chips
- 1/2 cup crushed graham crackers

Instructions:

1. Preheat the Oven:

- Preheat your oven to 325°F (163°C). Grease the bottom and sides of a 9-inch springform pan.

2. Prepare the Crust:

- In a bowl, mix graham cracker crumbs, melted butter, and sugar. Press the mixture into the bottom of the prepared springform pan to create a firm crust.

3. Bake the Crust:

- Bake the crust in the preheated oven for about 10 minutes. Remove from the oven and let it cool while preparing the filling.

4. Prepare the Cheesecake Filling:

- In a large mixing bowl, beat the softened cream cheese until smooth using an electric mixer.
- Add sugar, vanilla extract, and eggs one at a time, beating well after each addition.
- Mix in sour cream and chocolate chips. Beat until the batter is smooth and well blended.

5. Pour Filling onto the Crust:

- Pour the chocolate chip-flavored cheesecake filling over the baked crust in the springform pan.

6. Bake the Cheesecake:

- Bake in the preheated oven for about 1 hour or until the center is set and the top is lightly browned.

7. Prepare the Topping:

- Sprinkle mini marshmallows, chocolate chips, and crushed graham crackers over the top of the baked cheesecake.

8. Broil the Topping:

- Preheat your broiler. Place the cheesecake with the topping under the broiler for a short time until the marshmallows are toasted and golden brown. Keep a close eye to prevent burning.

9. Cool and Refrigerate:

- Allow the cheesecake to cool in the pan on a wire rack. Once it reaches room temperature, cover and refrigerate for at least 4 hours or overnight.

10. Serve:

    - Before serving, run a knife around the edge of the pan to loosen the cheesecake. Remove the sides of the springform pan.
    - Slice and enjoy this S'mores Cheesecake, a delightful combination of creamy cheesecake, chocolate, and toasted marshmallows reminiscent of a classic campfire treat!

Raspberry Lemonade Cheesecake

Ingredients:

For the Crust:

- 2 cups graham cracker crumbs
- 1/2 cup melted unsalted butter
- 2 tablespoons sugar

For the Raspberry Lemonade Filling:

- 4 packages (32 ounces) cream cheese, softened
- 1 cup sugar
- 4 large eggs, room temperature
- 1 teaspoon vanilla extract
- Zest and juice of 3 lemons
- 1/2 cup raspberry puree (strained if desired)
- 1/4 cup all-purpose flour

For Raspberry Sauce:

- 1 cup fresh or frozen raspberries
- 2 tablespoons sugar
- 1 tablespoon lemon juice

For Garnish:

- Fresh raspberries
- Lemon slices
- Mint leaves

Instructions:

1. Preheat the Oven:

- Preheat your oven to 325°F (163°C). Grease the bottom and sides of a 9-inch springform pan.

2. Prepare the Crust:

- In a bowl, mix graham cracker crumbs, melted butter, and sugar. Press the mixture into the bottom of the prepared springform pan to create a firm crust.

3. Bake the Crust:

- Bake the crust in the preheated oven for about 10 minutes. Remove from the oven and let it cool while preparing the filling.

4. Prepare the Raspberry Lemonade Filling:

- In a large mixing bowl, beat the softened cream cheese until smooth using an electric mixer.
- Add sugar, vanilla extract, and eggs one at a time, beating well after each addition.
- Mix in lemon zest, lemon juice, raspberry puree, and flour. Beat until the batter is smooth and well blended.

5. Pour Filling onto the Crust:

- Pour the raspberry lemonade-flavored cheesecake filling over the baked crust in the springform pan.

6. Bake the Cheesecake:

- Bake in the preheated oven for about 1 hour or until the center is set and the top is lightly browned.

7. Prepare Raspberry Sauce:

- In a saucepan, combine raspberries, sugar, and lemon juice. Cook over medium heat until the raspberries break down and the sauce thickens. Strain if desired.

8. Cool and Refrigerate:

- Allow the cheesecake to cool in the pan on a wire rack. Once it reaches room temperature, cover and refrigerate for at least 4 hours or overnight.

9. Serve:

- Before serving, run a knife around the edge of the pan to loosen the cheesecake. Remove the sides of the springform pan.
- Drizzle each slice with raspberry sauce and garnish with fresh raspberries, lemon slices, and mint leaves.

10. Enjoy:

- Slice and enjoy this Raspberry Lemonade Cheesecake, a delightful and zesty dessert perfect for a summer treat!

Turtle Cheesecake

Ingredients:

For the Crust:

- 2 cups chocolate cookie crumbs
- 1/2 cup melted unsalted butter
- 2 tablespoons sugar

For the Cheesecake Filling:

- 4 packages (32 ounces) cream cheese, softened
- 1 cup sugar
- 4 large eggs, room temperature
- 1 teaspoon vanilla extract
- 1/4 cup all-purpose flour
- 1/2 cup caramel sauce (plus extra for topping)
- 1/2 cup chopped pecans

For the Topping:

- 1 cup chocolate chips
- 1/2 cup chopped pecans

Instructions:

1. Preheat the Oven:

   - Preheat your oven to 325°F (163°C). Grease the bottom and sides of a 9-inch springform pan.

2. Prepare the Crust:

   - In a bowl, mix chocolate cookie crumbs, melted butter, and sugar. Press the mixture into the bottom of the prepared springform pan to create a firm crust.

3. Bake the Crust:

- Bake the crust in the preheated oven for about 10 minutes. Remove from the oven and let it cool while preparing the filling.

4. Prepare the Cheesecake Filling:

- In a large mixing bowl, beat the softened cream cheese until smooth using an electric mixer.
- Add sugar, vanilla extract, and eggs one at a time, beating well after each addition.
- Mix in flour, caramel sauce, and chopped pecans. Beat until the batter is smooth and well blended.

5. Pour Filling onto the Crust:

- Pour the caramel and pecan-flavored cheesecake filling over the baked crust in the springform pan.

6. Bake the Cheesecake:

- Bake in the preheated oven for about 1 hour or until the center is set and the top is lightly browned.

7. Prepare the Topping:

- In a microwave-safe bowl, melt the chocolate chips in 30-second intervals, stirring between each interval until smooth.
- Pour the melted chocolate over the top of the baked cheesecake and spread it evenly.
- Sprinkle chopped pecans over the melted chocolate.

8. Cool and Refrigerate:

- Allow the cheesecake to cool in the pan on a wire rack. Once it reaches room temperature, cover and refrigerate for at least 4 hours or overnight.

9. Serve:

- Before serving, run a knife around the edge of the pan to loosen the cheesecake. Remove the sides of the springform pan.
- Drizzle additional caramel sauce over the top if desired.

10. Enjoy:

    - Slice and enjoy this Turtle Cheesecake, a rich and indulgent dessert with the classic combination of chocolate, caramel, and pecans!

Almond Amaretto Cheesecake

Ingredients:

For the Almond Graham Cracker Crust:

- 2 cups graham cracker crumbs
- 1/2 cup melted unsalted butter
- 1/2 cup ground almonds
- 2 tablespoons sugar

For the Cheesecake Filling:

- 4 packages (32 ounces) cream cheese, softened
- 1 cup sugar
- 4 large eggs, room temperature
- 1 teaspoon almond extract
- 1/4 cup amaretto liqueur
- 1/4 cup all-purpose flour
- 1/2 cup sour cream

For the Almond Amaretto Topping:

- 1/2 cup sliced almonds, toasted
- 1/4 cup amaretto liqueur
- 1/4 cup sugar

Instructions:

1. Preheat the Oven:

- Preheat your oven to 325°F (163°C). Grease the bottom and sides of a 9-inch springform pan.

2. Prepare the Almond Graham Cracker Crust:

- In a bowl, mix graham cracker crumbs, melted butter, ground almonds, and sugar. Press the mixture into the bottom of the prepared springform pan to create a firm crust.

3. Bake the Crust:

- Bake the crust in the preheated oven for about 10 minutes. Remove from the oven and let it cool while preparing the filling.

4. Prepare the Cheesecake Filling:

- In a large mixing bowl, beat the softened cream cheese until smooth using an electric mixer.
- Add sugar, almond extract, and amaretto liqueur. Beat until well combined.
- Add eggs one at a time, beating well after each addition.
- Mix in flour and sour cream. Beat until the batter is smooth and well blended.

5. Pour Filling onto the Crust:

- Pour the almond amaretto-flavored cheesecake filling over the baked crust in the springform pan.

6. Bake the Cheesecake:

- Bake in the preheated oven for about 1 hour or until the center is set and the top is lightly browned.

7. Prepare the Almond Amaretto Topping:

- In a small saucepan, heat amaretto liqueur and sugar until the sugar dissolves and the mixture thickens slightly.
- Toast sliced almonds in a dry skillet until golden brown.

8. Apply the Topping:

- Once the cheesecake has cooled slightly, pour the amaretto syrup over the top and sprinkle toasted sliced almonds.

9. Cool and Refrigerate:

- Allow the cheesecake to cool in the pan on a wire rack. Once it reaches room temperature, cover and refrigerate for at least 4 hours or overnight.

10. Serve:

- Before serving, run a knife around the edge of the pan to loosen the cheesecake. Remove the sides of the springform pan.
- Slice and savor this Almond Amaretto Cheesecake, a delightful dessert with the rich flavors of almonds and amaretto!

Chocolate Covered Strawberry Cheesecake

Ingredients:

For the Chocolate Cookie Crust:

- 2 cups chocolate cookie crumbs
- 1/2 cup melted unsalted butter
- 2 tablespoons sugar

For the Cheesecake Filling:

- 4 packages (32 ounces) cream cheese, softened
- 1 cup sugar
- 4 large eggs, room temperature
- 1 teaspoon vanilla extract
- 1/2 cup sour cream
- 1/2 cup strawberry puree (fresh or frozen strawberries blended)

For the Chocolate Ganache Topping:

- 1 cup semisweet chocolate chips
- 1/2 cup heavy cream

For Garnish:

- Fresh strawberries, halved or sliced

Instructions:

1. Preheat the Oven:

- Preheat your oven to 325°F (163°C). Grease the bottom and sides of a 9-inch springform pan.

2. Prepare the Chocolate Cookie Crust:

- In a bowl, mix chocolate cookie crumbs, melted butter, and sugar. Press the mixture into the bottom of the prepared springform pan to create a firm crust.

3. Bake the Crust:

- Bake the crust in the preheated oven for about 10 minutes. Remove from the oven and let it cool while preparing the filling.

4. Prepare the Cheesecake Filling:

- In a large mixing bowl, beat the softened cream cheese until smooth using an electric mixer.
- Add sugar, vanilla extract, and eggs one at a time, beating well after each addition.
- Mix in sour cream and strawberry puree. Beat until the batter is smooth and well blended.

5. Pour Filling onto the Crust:

- Pour the strawberry-flavored cheesecake filling over the baked crust in the springform pan.

6. Bake the Cheesecake:

- Bake in the preheated oven for about 1 hour or until the center is set and the top is lightly browned.

7. Prepare the Chocolate Ganache Topping:

- In a small saucepan, heat the heavy cream until it's just about to boil. Remove from heat and add chocolate chips. Stir until smooth and well combined.

8. Pour Ganache over Cheesecake:

- Pour the chocolate ganache over the top of the baked cheesecake, spreading it evenly.

9. Chill:

- Allow the cheesecake to cool in the pan on a wire rack. Once it reaches room temperature, cover and refrigerate for at least 4 hours or overnight.

10. Garnish and Serve:

- Before serving, garnish the cheesecake with fresh strawberry slices.
- Slice and enjoy this Chocolate Covered Strawberry Cheesecake, a luscious combination of creamy cheesecake, chocolate, and strawberries!

Brownie Bottom Cheesecake

Ingredients:

For the Brownie Bottom:

- 1 box (18-20 ounces) brownie mix (plus ingredients mentioned on the box)

For the Cheesecake Filling:

- 4 packages (32 ounces) cream cheese, softened
- 1 cup sugar
- 4 large eggs, room temperature
- 1 teaspoon vanilla extract
- 1/2 cup sour cream

For Garnish:

- Chocolate ganache (optional)
- Whipped cream (optional)

Instructions:

1. Preheat the Oven:

- Preheat your oven to the temperature specified on the brownie mix box. Grease the bottom and sides of a 9-inch springform pan.

2. Prepare the Brownie Bottom:

- Prepare the brownie mix according to the package instructions.
- Pour the brownie batter into the prepared springform pan, spreading it evenly on the bottom.
- Bake the brownie layer according to the package instructions. Keep in mind that the brownie will continue to bake with the cheesecake layer.

3. Prepare the Cheesecake Filling:

- In a large mixing bowl, beat the softened cream cheese until smooth using an electric mixer.
- Add sugar, vanilla extract, and eggs one at a time, beating well after each addition.
- Mix in sour cream. Beat until the batter is smooth and well blended.

4. Pour Filling onto the Brownie Bottom:

- Pour the cheesecake filling over the baked brownie layer in the springform pan.

5. Bake the Cheesecake:

- Bake in the preheated oven for about 1 hour or until the center is set and the top is lightly browned.

6. Cool and Chill:

- Allow the cheesecake to cool in the pan on a wire rack. Once it reaches room temperature, cover and refrigerate for at least 4 hours or overnight.

7. Optional Chocolate Ganache:

- If desired, you can drizzle the top with chocolate ganache for an extra chocolatey touch.

8. Garnish and Serve:

- Before serving, you can garnish the cheesecake with whipped cream or any other desired toppings.
- Slice and enjoy this Brownie Bottom Cheesecake, a delightful combination of rich brownie and creamy cheesecake!

Snickers Cheesecake

Ingredients:

For the Crust:

- 2 cups chocolate cookie crumbs
- 1/2 cup melted unsalted butter
- 2 tablespoons sugar

For the Cheesecake Filling:

- 4 packages (32 ounces) cream cheese, softened
- 1 cup sugar
- 4 large eggs, room temperature
- 1 teaspoon vanilla extract
- 1/2 cup sour cream
- 1 cup chopped Snickers bars

For the Caramel Sauce:

- 1 cup caramel candies, unwrapped
- 1/4 cup heavy cream

For the Chocolate Ganache:

- 1 cup semisweet chocolate chips
- 1/2 cup heavy cream

For Garnish:

- Chopped Snickers bars
- Additional caramel sauce

Instructions:

1. Preheat the Oven:

    - Preheat your oven to 325°F (163°C). Grease the bottom and sides of a 9-inch springform pan.

2. Prepare the Crust:

    - In a bowl, mix chocolate cookie crumbs, melted butter, and sugar. Press the mixture into the bottom of the prepared springform pan to create a firm crust.

3. Bake the Crust:

    - Bake the crust in the preheated oven for about 10 minutes. Remove from the oven and let it cool while preparing the filling.

4. Prepare the Cheesecake Filling:

    - In a large mixing bowl, beat the softened cream cheese until smooth using an electric mixer.
    - Add sugar, vanilla extract, and eggs one at a time, beating well after each addition.
    - Mix in sour cream and chopped Snickers bars. Beat until the batter is smooth and well blended.

5. Pour Filling onto the Crust:

    - Pour the Snickers-flavored cheesecake filling over the baked crust in the springform pan.

6. Bake the Cheesecake:

    - Bake in the preheated oven for about 1 hour or until the center is set and the top is lightly browned.

7. Prepare the Caramel Sauce:

- In a saucepan, melt caramel candies with heavy cream over medium heat, stirring until smooth. Set aside.

8. Prepare the Chocolate Ganache:

    - In another saucepan, heat chocolate chips and heavy cream over low heat, stirring until smooth. Set aside.

9. Apply the Toppings:

    - Once the cheesecake has cooled slightly, drizzle caramel sauce over the top.
    - Pour chocolate ganache over the caramel layer.
    - Sprinkle chopped Snickers bars over the top.

10. Cool and Refrigerate:

    - Allow the cheesecake to cool in the pan on a wire rack. Once it reaches room temperature, cover and refrigerate for at least 4 hours or overnight.

11. Serve:

    - Before serving, run a knife around the edge of the pan to loosen the cheesecake. Remove the sides of the springform pan.
    - Drizzle additional caramel sauce over individual slices if desired.

12. Enjoy:

    - Slice and indulge in this Snickers Cheesecake, a heavenly combination of creamy cheesecake, caramel, chocolate, and Snickers goodness!

Cinnamon Roll Cheesecake

Ingredients:

For the Cinnamon Roll Crust:

- 2 cups cinnamon roll crumbs (you can use store-bought or homemade)
- 1/2 cup melted unsalted butter

For the Cheesecake Filling:

- 4 packages (32 ounces) cream cheese, softened
- 1 cup sugar
- 4 large eggs, room temperature
- 1 teaspoon vanilla extract
- 1/2 cup sour cream

For the Cinnamon Swirl:

- 1/4 cup sugar
- 2 teaspoons ground cinnamon

For the Cream Cheese Frosting:

- 4 ounces cream cheese, softened
- 1/4 cup unsalted butter, softened
- 1 cup powdered sugar
- 1/2 teaspoon vanilla extract

Instructions:

1. Preheat the Oven:

- Preheat your oven to 325°F (163°C). Grease the bottom and sides of a 9-inch springform pan.

2. Prepare the Cinnamon Roll Crust:

- In a bowl, mix cinnamon roll crumbs and melted butter. Press the mixture into the bottom of the prepared springform pan to create a firm crust.

3. Prepare the Cheesecake Filling:

- In a large mixing bowl, beat the softened cream cheese until smooth using an electric mixer.
- Add sugar, vanilla extract, and eggs one at a time, beating well after each addition.
- Mix in sour cream. Beat until the batter is smooth and well blended.

4. Pour Filling onto the Crust:

- Pour half of the cheesecake filling over the cinnamon roll crust in the springform pan.

5. Prepare the Cinnamon Swirl:

- In a small bowl, mix sugar and ground cinnamon. Sprinkle half of this mixture over the cheesecake filling in the pan.
- Pour the remaining cheesecake filling over the cinnamon swirl layer.
- Sprinkle the remaining cinnamon swirl mixture on top.

6. Swirl the Batter:

- Use a knife or skewer to gently swirl the cinnamon mixture into the cheesecake batter for a marbled effect.

7. Bake the Cheesecake:

- Bake in the preheated oven for about 1 hour or until the center is set and the top is lightly browned.

8. Prepare the Cream Cheese Frosting:

- In a bowl, beat together softened cream cheese, softened butter, powdered sugar, and vanilla extract until smooth.

9. Cool and Chill:

- Allow the cheesecake to cool in the pan on a wire rack. Once it reaches room temperature, cover and refrigerate for at least 4 hours or overnight.

10. Frost and Serve:

- Before serving, spread the cream cheese frosting over the top of the chilled cheesecake.
- Slice and enjoy this Cinnamon Roll Cheesecake, a heavenly treat that combines the flavors of a classic cinnamon roll with creamy cheesecake!

Chocolate Mousse Cheesecake

Ingredients:

For the Chocolate Cookie Crust:

- 2 cups chocolate cookie crumbs
- 1/2 cup melted unsalted butter
- 2 tablespoons sugar

For the Cheesecake Filling:

- 4 packages (32 ounces) cream cheese, softened
- 1 cup sugar
- 4 large eggs, room temperature
- 1 teaspoon vanilla extract
- 1/2 cup sour cream

For the Chocolate Mousse Layer:

- 1 1/2 cups semisweet chocolate chips
- 1 1/2 cups heavy cream
- 1/4 cup powdered sugar
- 1 teaspoon vanilla extract

For Garnish:

- Whipped cream
- Chocolate shavings or curls

Instructions:

1. Preheat the Oven:

- Preheat your oven to 325°F (163°C). Grease the bottom and sides of a 9-inch springform pan.

2. Prepare the Chocolate Cookie Crust:

- In a bowl, mix chocolate cookie crumbs, melted butter, and sugar. Press the mixture into the bottom of the prepared springform pan to create a firm crust.

3. Bake the Crust:

    - Bake the crust in the preheated oven for about 10 minutes. Remove from the oven and let it cool while preparing the filling.

4. Prepare the Cheesecake Filling:

    - In a large mixing bowl, beat the softened cream cheese until smooth using an electric mixer.
    - Add sugar, vanilla extract, and eggs one at a time, beating well after each addition.
    - Mix in sour cream. Beat until the batter is smooth and well blended.

5. Pour Filling onto the Crust:

    - Pour the cheesecake filling over the baked crust in the springform pan.

6. Bake the Cheesecake:

    - Bake in the preheated oven for about 1 hour or until the center is set and the top is lightly browned.

7. Prepare the Chocolate Mousse Layer:

    - In a heatproof bowl, melt the chocolate chips over a double boiler or in the microwave.
    - In a separate bowl, whip the heavy cream, powdered sugar, and vanilla extract until stiff peaks form.
    - Gently fold the melted chocolate into the whipped cream until well combined.

8. Apply the Mousse Layer:

    - Once the cheesecake has cooled slightly, spread the chocolate mousse layer evenly over the top.

9. Chill:

- Allow the cheesecake to cool completely, then cover and refrigerate for at least 4 hours or overnight.

10. Garnish and Serve:

    - Before serving, garnish the cheesecake with whipped cream and chocolate shavings or curls.
    - Slice and enjoy this Chocolate Mousse Cheesecake, a decadent dessert that combines the rich flavors of chocolate and creamy cheesecake!

Blueberry Lemon Cheesecake Bars

Ingredients:

For the Crust:

- 1 1/2 cups graham cracker crumbs
- 1/3 cup melted unsalted butter
- 2 tablespoons sugar

For the Cheesecake Filling:

- 2 packages (16 ounces each) cream cheese, softened
- 1 cup sugar
- 3 large eggs
- 1 teaspoon vanilla extract
- Zest of 1 lemon
- 2 tablespoons fresh lemon juice
- 1/4 cup all-purpose flour

For the Blueberry Swirl:

- 1 cup fresh or frozen blueberries
- 2 tablespoons sugar
- 1 tablespoon water
- 1 tablespoon lemon juice
- 1 teaspoon cornstarch mixed with 1 tablespoon water (for thickening)

Instructions:

1. Preheat the Oven:

- Preheat your oven to 325°F (163°C). Line a 9x13-inch baking pan with parchment paper, leaving an overhang on the sides for easy removal.

2. Prepare the Crust:

- In a bowl, mix graham cracker crumbs, melted butter, and sugar. Press the mixture into the bottom of the prepared baking pan to create a firm crust.

3. Bake the Crust:

- Bake the crust in the preheated oven for about 10 minutes. Remove from the oven and let it cool while preparing the filling.

4. Prepare the Cheesecake Filling:

- In a large mixing bowl, beat the softened cream cheese until smooth using an electric mixer.
- Add sugar, eggs, vanilla extract, lemon zest, lemon juice, and flour. Beat until the batter is smooth and well blended.

5. Pour Filling onto the Crust:

- Pour the cheesecake filling over the baked crust in the prepared baking pan.

6. Prepare the Blueberry Swirl:

- In a saucepan, combine blueberries, sugar, water, and lemon juice. Cook over medium heat until the blueberries burst and release their juices.
- Stir in the cornstarch-water mixture and continue cooking until the mixture thickens. Remove from heat.

7. Swirl Blueberry Mixture:

- Drop spoonfuls of the blueberry mixture onto the cheesecake batter. Use a knife to swirl the blueberry mixture into the cheesecake batter for a marbled effect.

8. Bake the Cheesecake Bars:

- Bake in the preheated oven for about 25-30 minutes or until the edges are set, and the center is slightly jiggly.

9. Cool and Chill:

- Allow the cheesecake bars to cool in the pan on a wire rack. Once it reaches room temperature, cover and refrigerate for at least 4 hours or overnight.

10. Slice and Serve:

- Use the parchment paper overhangs to lift the cheesecake bars from the pan. Cut into squares and serve.

11. Enjoy:

- Enjoy these refreshing Blueberry Lemon Cheesecake Bars, perfect for a summer treat or any special occasion!

Marble Cheesecake

Ingredients:

For the Crust:

- 1 1/2 cups graham cracker crumbs
- 1/4 cup melted unsalted butter
- 2 tablespoons sugar

For the Cheesecake Filling:

- 4 packages (32 ounces) cream cheese, softened
- 1 cup sugar
- 4 large eggs, room temperature
- 1 teaspoon vanilla extract

For the Chocolate Swirl:

- 1/2 cup semisweet chocolate chips, melted
- 2 tablespoons unsweetened cocoa powder
- 2 tablespoons sugar

Instructions:

1. Preheat the Oven:

- Preheat your oven to 325°F (163°C). Grease the bottom and sides of a 9-inch springform pan.

2. Prepare the Crust:

- In a bowl, mix graham cracker crumbs, melted butter, and sugar. Press the mixture into the bottom of the prepared springform pan to create a firm crust.

3. Bake the Crust:

- Bake the crust in the preheated oven for about 10 minutes. Remove from the oven and let it cool while preparing the filling.

4. Prepare the Cheesecake Filling:

- In a large mixing bowl, beat the softened cream cheese until smooth using an electric mixer.
- Add sugar, vanilla extract, and eggs one at a time, beating well after each addition.

5. Create the Chocolate Swirl:

- In a small bowl, mix melted chocolate, cocoa powder, and sugar until well combined.

6. Assemble the Cheesecake:

- Pour half of the cream cheese filling over the baked crust.
- Spoon dollops of the chocolate swirl mixture onto the cream cheese layer.
- Use a knife to gently swirl the chocolate mixture into the cream cheese mixture for a marbled effect.
- Pour the remaining cream cheese filling over the top.
- Repeat the swirling process with the remaining chocolate mixture.

7. Bake the Cheesecake:

- Bake in the preheated oven for about 1 hour or until the center is set and the top is lightly browned.

8. Cool and Chill:

- Allow the cheesecake to cool in the pan on a wire rack. Once it reaches room temperature, cover and refrigerate for at least 4 hours or overnight.

9. Serve:

- Before serving, run a knife around the edge of the pan to loosen the cheesecake. Remove the sides of the springform pan.
- Slice and enjoy this Marble Cheesecake, a delightful combination of vanilla and chocolate swirls in a creamy cheesecake!

Raspberry Cheesecake Ice Cream

Ingredients:

- 1 cup fresh or frozen raspberries
- 1/4 cup sugar
- 1 tablespoon lemon juice

For the Cheesecake Ice Cream Base:

- 2 cups heavy cream
- 1 cup whole milk
- 1 cup sugar
- 4 ounces cream cheese, softened
- 1 teaspoon vanilla extract

For the Cheesecake Swirl:

- 4 ounces cream cheese, softened
- 1/4 cup powdered sugar
- 1/2 teaspoon vanilla extract

Instructions:

1. Prepare the Raspberry Sauce:

- In a small saucepan, combine raspberries, sugar, and lemon juice. Cook over medium heat until the raspberries break down and the mixture thickens. Remove from heat and let it cool.

2. Make the Cheesecake Ice Cream Base:

- In a mixing bowl, beat the softened cream cheese until smooth.
- Add sugar and continue to beat until well combined.
- Pour in the heavy cream, whole milk, and vanilla extract. Mix until the sugar is fully dissolved.
- Transfer the mixture to an ice cream maker and churn according to the manufacturer's instructions.

3. Prepare the Cheesecake Swirl:

- In a separate bowl, beat together the cream cheese, powdered sugar, and vanilla extract until smooth and creamy.

4. Assemble the Ice Cream:

    - Once the ice cream has reached a soft-serve consistency, layer it in a container with spoonfuls of the raspberry sauce and dollops of the cheesecake swirl.
    - Repeat the layers until all the ingredients are used.
    - Use a knife or skewer to gently swirl the raspberry sauce and cheesecake mixture into the ice cream.

5. Freeze:

    - Cover the container with a lid or plastic wrap and freeze the ice cream for at least 4 hours or overnight to firm up.

6. Serve:

    - Scoop and serve this delightful Raspberry Cheesecake Ice Cream in cones or bowls.

Enjoy the creamy goodness with swirls of raspberry and cheesecake in every bite!

Pineapple Upside-Down Cheesecake

Ingredients:

For the Pineapple Topping:

- 1/2 cup unsalted butter
- 1 cup packed brown sugar
- 1 can (20 ounces) pineapple slices, drained
- Maraschino cherries for garnish

For the Cheesecake Filling:

- 4 packages (32 ounces) cream cheese, softened
- 1 cup sugar
- 4 large eggs, room temperature
- 1 teaspoon vanilla extract
- 1/2 cup sour cream

For the Crust:

- 1 1/2 cups graham cracker crumbs
- 1/4 cup melted butter

Instructions:

1. Preheat the Oven:

- Preheat your oven to 325°F (163°C). Grease the bottom and sides of a 9-inch springform pan.

2. Prepare the Pineapple Topping:

- In a saucepan, melt the butter over medium heat. Add the brown sugar and stir until well combined.
- Pour the butter and sugar mixture into the bottom of the prepared springform pan.
- Arrange pineapple slices on top of the butter and sugar mixture. Place maraschino cherries in the center of each pineapple slice.

3. Prepare the Cheesecake Filling:

   - In a large mixing bowl, beat the softened cream cheese until smooth using an electric mixer.
   - Add sugar, vanilla extract, and eggs one at a time, beating well after each addition.
   - Mix in sour cream. Beat until the batter is smooth and well blended.

4. Prepare the Crust:

   - In a small bowl, mix graham cracker crumbs and melted butter. Press the mixture onto the pineapple layer in the springform pan.

5. Pour Filling onto the Crust:

   - Pour the cheesecake filling over the graham cracker crust in the springform pan.

6. Bake the Cheesecake:

   - Bake in the preheated oven for about 1 hour or until the center is set and the top is lightly browned.

7. Cool and Chill:

   - Allow the cheesecake to cool in the pan on a wire rack. Once it reaches room temperature, cover and refrigerate for at least 4 hours or overnight.

8. Serve:

   - Before serving, run a knife around the edge of the pan to loosen the cheesecake. Remove the sides of the springform pan.
   - Invert the cheesecake onto a serving platter, so the pineapple topping is on top.
   - Slice and enjoy this Pineapple Upside-Down Cheesecake, a delightful twist on the classic dessert!

Matcha Green Tea Cheesecake

Ingredients:

For the Crust:

- 1 1/2 cups graham cracker crumbs
- 1/4 cup melted unsalted butter
- 2 tablespoons sugar

For the Matcha Cheesecake Filling:

- 4 packages (32 ounces) cream cheese, softened
- 1 cup sugar
- 4 large eggs, room temperature
- 1 teaspoon vanilla extract
- 1/4 cup all-purpose flour
- 2 tablespoons matcha green tea powder

For the Matcha Swirl:

- 2 teaspoons matcha green tea powder
- 2 tablespoons hot water
- 1 tablespoon sugar

Instructions:

1. Preheat the Oven:

- Preheat your oven to 325°F (163°C). Grease the bottom and sides of a 9-inch springform pan.

2. Prepare the Crust:

- In a bowl, mix graham cracker crumbs, melted butter, and sugar. Press the mixture into the bottom of the prepared springform pan to create a firm crust.

3. Bake the Crust:

- Bake the crust in the preheated oven for about 10 minutes. Remove from the oven and let it cool while preparing the filling.

4. Prepare the Matcha Cheesecake Filling:

- In a large mixing bowl, beat the softened cream cheese until smooth using an electric mixer.
- Add sugar, vanilla extract, and eggs one at a time, beating well after each addition.
- Mix in flour and matcha green tea powder until the batter is smooth and well blended.

5. Prepare the Matcha Swirl:

- In a small bowl, dissolve matcha green tea powder in hot water. Stir in sugar until well combined.

6. Assemble the Cheesecake:

- Pour the matcha cheesecake filling over the baked crust in the springform pan.
- Spoon dollops of the matcha swirl mixture onto the cheesecake layer.
- Use a knife or skewer to gently swirl the matcha mixture into the cheesecake batter for a marbled effect.

7. Bake the Cheesecake:

- Bake in the preheated oven for about 1 hour or until the center is set and the top is lightly browned.

8. Cool and Chill:

- Allow the cheesecake to cool in the pan on a wire rack. Once it reaches room temperature, cover and refrigerate for at least 4 hours or overnight.

9. Serve:

- Before serving, run a knife around the edge of the pan to loosen the cheesecake. Remove the sides of the springform pan.
- Slice and enjoy this Matcha Green Tea Cheesecake, a unique and flavorful twist on the classic dessert!

Fig and Honey Cheesecake

Ingredients:

For the Crust:

- 1 1/2 cups graham cracker crumbs
- 1/4 cup melted unsalted butter
- 2 tablespoons honey

For the Cheesecake Filling:

- 4 packages (32 ounces) cream cheese, softened
- 1 cup sugar
- 4 large eggs, room temperature
- 1 teaspoon vanilla extract
- 1/4 cup honey
- 1/2 cup sour cream

For the Fig Topping:

- 1 cup fresh figs, sliced
- 2 tablespoons honey
- 1/4 cup water

Instructions:

1. Preheat the Oven:

- Preheat your oven to 325°F (163°C). Grease the bottom and sides of a 9-inch springform pan.

2. Prepare the Crust:

- In a bowl, mix graham cracker crumbs, melted butter, and honey. Press the mixture into the bottom of the prepared springform pan to create a firm crust.

3. Bake the Crust:

- Bake the crust in the preheated oven for about 10 minutes. Remove from the oven and let it cool while preparing the filling.

4. Prepare the Cheesecake Filling:

- In a large mixing bowl, beat the softened cream cheese until smooth using an electric mixer.
- Add sugar, vanilla extract, honey, and eggs one at a time, beating well after each addition.
- Mix in sour cream until the batter is smooth and well blended.

5. Pour Filling onto the Crust:

- Pour the cheesecake filling over the baked crust in the springform pan.

6. Bake the Cheesecake:

- Bake in the preheated oven for about 1 hour or until the center is set and the top is lightly browned.

7. Prepare the Fig Topping:

- In a small saucepan, combine figs, honey, and water. Simmer over medium heat until the figs soften and the mixture thickens slightly.
- Let the fig topping cool.

8. Apply the Fig Topping:

- Once the cheesecake has cooled slightly, spread the fig topping over the top.

9. Chill:

- Allow the cheesecake to cool completely, then cover and refrigerate for at least 4 hours or overnight.

10. Serve:

    - Before serving, run a knife around the edge of the pan to loosen the cheesecake. Remove the sides of the springform pan.
    - Slice and enjoy this Fig and Honey Cheesecake, a delightful combination of creamy cheesecake with the natural sweetness of honey and figs!

www.ingramcontent.com/pod-product-compliance
Lightning Source LLC
LaVergne TN
LVHW081552060526
838201LV00054B/1864